# EDGE HILL
# UNIVERSITY COLLEGE
## A History
## 1885-1997

# EDGE HILL
# UNIVERSITY COLLEGE
## A History
## 1885-1997

Fiona A. Montgomery

Phillimore

1997

Published by
PHILLIMORE & CO. LTD.
Shopwyke Manor Barn, Chichester, West Sussex

ISBN 1 86077 042 8 (cased)
ISBN 1 86077 063 0 (limp)

Pirnted and bound in Great Britain by
BUTLER AND TANNER LTD.
London and Frome

# CONTENTS

# PREFACE

The years since 1985 have seen substantial change in the structure of higher education within the U.K. Shifts in access patterns, teaching methods and funding have meant challenge and tension between the past and the future. For this reason, it was decided to update Edge Hill's history, to demonstrate the ways in which it responded to the diversity of transformations which were taking place. It is interesting to note that the section from 1985 is almost as long as that covering the previous hundred years! The first seven chapters have been revised and new material added.

Once again, I am indebted to many people. As well as those thanked in the first edition, I would like to include: my family; Simon Brew, Alumni Officer who tirelessly sought out material; Josie Ball who was the only person who knew where some of the data was; Rhiannon Evans who initiated the book and gave encouragement; John Cater, Mark Flinn, Bob Wilson, Brian Greaves, Ruth Gee, Joe McNamara, Mike Frain, Ruth Jenkinson, Margaret Entwistle, Freda Bridge, Ann Smith, Catherine Shields, Jim Gorman who provided oral interviews; Eirlys Chinn, Shirley Morgan, Rita Davies; Gill Ashworth and other library staff who 'exhumed' photographs; Richard Foster, Barbara Smith, Sue Ainslie, Judith Webster, Elizabeth Wiredu, John Townsend, Terry Kershaw, Rachel Robinson, Andy Shaw, Tom Titherington, Ann Chapman, John Diamond, Phil Scraton and Angela Court. If I have omitted anyone, I apologise. Recent photographs appear by kind permission of Jonathan Keenan Photography (assisted by Nick Hunt), Roger Sinek, Nonconform, Rod Pye and Simon Brew.

Finally I would like to thank Judith Briggs who heroically typed this manuscript and provided help and encouragement in so many ways.

FIONA MONTGOMERY

# PREFACE
## TO THE FIRST EDITION

The idea of a publication to mark the centenary of the founding of Edge Hill College was first suggested to me by the then Director, Miss Marjorie Stantan. Preliminary research confirmed that this would be a worthwhile and interesting project, throwing light on both teacher education and the wider social history of the period with relevance also for those concerned with women's studies.

This work, then, aims to present both a readable account of the last hundred years and to fill one of the many gaps in the published history of Education. Those who have less interest in educational policy might perhaps find the sections on 'College Life' more to their liking. With this in mind and for reasons of cost, footnotes have been kept to a minimum, and the Bibliography contains only a small selection of the material consulted. Nor is there any detailed discussion of any one specific department or subject.

A wide variety of contemporary sources including oral evidence has been consulted. The Edge Hill archives have many deficiencies: first, there are large gaps; second, though registers of students are extant, they give much less information than those existing for some other colleges—there is for example nothing on the occupations of students' fathers thus making it impossible to say anything precise about social class; third, there is much inconsistency in the way material is presented, thereby ensuring that what should be simple tasks, such as finding students' places or origin, becomes a lengthy business. These problems did not end with the modern period: access to material from the last twenty years has been limited and inconsistency again is evident.

Many have given help and encouragement in overcoming these obstacles. I am much indebted to all the members of the Guild who in providing reminiscences have given life to the volume: Miss Stella Evans, Mrs. E.G. Price, Mrs. E.M. Duckworth, Mrs. M. Bradley, Mrs. Eve Johnson, Mrs. N. Howie, Mrs. A. Bradshaw, Mrs. M. Aldred, Miss V. Berry, Mrs. G. Newsham, Mrs. C. Campbell, Mrs. O. Bryson, Mrs. E. Wilkinson, Mrs. G. Cadenhead, Miss M.C. Blythe, Miss M.C. English, Mrs. D.M. Fox, Mrs. R. Breese, Mrs. E. Ryley, Mrs. A. M. Laing, Mrs. K. Dowson, Miss H.E. Tuer, Mrs. M.J. Hennessey—if I have omitted anyone I apologise. I should also like to thank the following: Dr. F.V. Parsons, Reader in History, University of Glasgow, read the typescript, Mrs. E. Hannavy and the Library staff, Mrs. V. Harrhy kindly allowed me access to her two unpublished essays on the 'History of PE at Edge Hill', Dr. B. Greaves helped smooth out many problems, Mr. R. Pye produced the photographs, Miss J. Ball typed the manuscript with her usual efficiency, Mr. B. Cook allowed me to use one of his excellent cartoons, Mr. B. Horn, Mr. L. Ruscoe, Mr. F.W. Stacey, Mr. R. Slatter, Miss Bampton and all others who provided information and support.

Since this book has been researched and written purely in my own time, all my family, especially my husband Dr. David Halsall has tolerated the endless nights spent on it with surprising patience, my husband also having provided invaluable help with the proof-reading. The opinions are of course my own.

FIONA A. MONTGOMERY
March 1985

*For my family*

# 1
# ORIGINS

There can be no doubt that for many years after the establishment of a national system of elementary education by the Act of 1870, the supply of trained teachers fell far below the needs of the country.[1]

The 1870 Education Act gave rise to a rapid increase in the number of public elementary schools and a corresponding need for more teachers. Most teachers undertook an 'apprenticeship period' of five years as a pupil teacher and then perhaps attended a training college.[2] Such institutions were overwhelmingly denominational (35 out of 41 in 1880) and Anglican in character. This lack of non-denominational training was behind the move on 7 February 1882 of seven Liverpool businessmen and philanthropists—Alexander Balfour, Thomas Matheson, Samuel Smith, William Crosfield, W.P. Sinclair, S. McDairmid and S.G. Rathbone (chairman of the Liverpool School Board)—to found the first non-denominational Teachers Training College in England and Wales. It was designed to meet a two-fold need: first, existing colleges had insufficient places for the numbers applying and this led many to become unqualified acting teachers, and second, the existing colleges being denominational gave preference to students of their religious persuasion. 'Members of churches to which no college is attached who desire a college training, are thus placed at a disadvantage.'[3] A further reason, unstated, but no doubt of influence to the group, was the fact that headships were restricted to college-trained teachers, thus effectively cutting out non-Anglicans.

A committee was established, and after much effort and tireless fund raising a large house in Durning Road, Liverpool (previously occupied by George Holt) was secured. The building was furnished, adapted and enlarged by the addition of a new wing containing classrooms and dormitories. The cost was £16,483 of which over £10,000 was met by subscriptions.

The refitted basement of the original house accommodated the kitchen, serving rooms, sculleries, pantries, stores, servants hall and ironing room. The new wing had the dining room, principal's room, cloakroom, visitors' room and two classrooms on the ground floor. The first floor held the principal's and governesses' bedrooms and sitting rooms, bathroom and some student dormitories. The second floor was devoted to sleeping accommodation for students and servants. A small hospital was also incorporated in the building.

Originally the College was to be named 'Liverpool Undenominational College' and this had in fact been cut into the stone of the building. The Board of Education objected, however, because it feared that it might be confused with the existing Roman Catholic College in Mount Pleasant. As a result, 'Edge Hill', after the district in which it was sited, was chosen.

On 24 January 1885 Edge Hill was formally opened. A large meeting took place at St George's Hall, Liverpool attended by the Rt. Hon. G.O. Trevelyan, MP and J.G. Fitch, the Senior Inspector of Schools, both of whom delivered addresses extolling the value of training colleges and the need for trained teachers.

*1  Miss Sarah Yelf*                                    *2  Harriet D. Feuchsel*

Work now began in earnest. The staff consisted of the Principal, Miss Sarah Yelf, who had herself approached the committee and asked for the position, first governess Harriet D. Feuchsel, second governess Mildred Fenemore, third governess M.K. Dewhurst; Mrs. Evans, who taught cookery, and a number of visiting lecturers for such subjects as drawing and music. The appointment of a woman as principal was far in advance of official thinking; it was not till after 1904 that the regulations required a woman principal for a women's college. Miss Yelf had had a long career in education. Trained at Salisbury Diocesan Training College between 1861-2, she became headmistress of Teddington Church School on completion of her course and remained there for three years. How she managed to start at such a position is unknown. From 1865-76 she was second mistress at Salisbury College. In 1876 she became Inspectress of the Liverpool Board Schools and Principal of the Liverpool Pupil Teachers Centre for Girls. Miss Feuchsel had previously been a governess in Brighton Technical College; Miss Fenemore, headmistress of St Michael's Girls School, Highgate, while Miss Dewhurst came straight from Derby Training College.

In July 1884, 100 candidates had taken the Scholarship Examination and from these 41 became resident students at the end of January 1885. Edge Hill's intention was 'to produce a superior class of Elementary School Mistresses', thereby trying to create the impression that they were a cut above the ordinary Training College and perhaps responding to the wish to draw middle-class applicants into the profession. This was to be ensured by a 'careful selection' of suitable candidates and equipping them with an appropriate education.

As there were always many more applicants nationally than there were places, a college could pick and choose (the Board of Education had no say). Till 1899 all intending students had to pass the Queen's Scholarship Examination; candidates were arranged in order of merit and position on the list was very important. Interestingly, however, in listing the qualifications needed for admission, Edge Hill rated health first 'as to which the decision of the College

3   M.K. Dewhurst                    4   Kate Evans

Medical Officer is final'; then came position on the Queen's Scholarship List; character testimonials; 'previous success' in Drawing and Science; and a rather vague 'every other circumstance from which it may probably be inferred that the advantages bestowed in the College will lead to the desired result'. A good knowledge of French, German or Latin was 'desirable' while skill in needlework, domestic economy and music was 'indispensable'. Right from the start, then, Edge Hill was reflecting and reinforcing conventional gender roles with its interest in stereotypical conventional feminine skills, such as needlework and domestic economy. Teaching was seen as an extremely tiring occupation and one for which a woman had to be very fit.

Once accepted, students received a memorandum from the Principal telling them when to report to Edge Hill and what to bring with them. A comprehensive list was issued: a waterproof cloak, two pairs of stout walking boots, goloshes or rubbers, two pairs of shoes, dressing gown, flannel underclothing ('vests at least'), a white or cream dress, navy blue serge dress for school and classroom, aprons, two toilet covers, two bags for linen. For P.E. one cream and one crimson shirt blouse in 'Delaine' was required. This had to be made with 'yoke, turn down collar, and full sleeves with loosely fitting cuffs'. By 1912 these blouses had been dispensed with; the 'costume' now consisted of 'knickers, tunic and jersey' which had to be bought from Edge Hill 'to ensure uniformity'. A sailor hat with College band and badge was compulsory for weekday wear. All were 'expected to appear at all times neatly and becomingly attired'. Revaccination and 'teeth put in order' were also required.

Fees were: £10 for those who had been pupil teachers and had first-class Queen's Scholarships, £12 for those in the second class. If the student had not been a pupil teacher, fees were £15 for the first-class scholarship holder and £20 for the second.

Edge Hill quickly established itself in a position of strength. Within five years it was ranked in the first class and it used this fact to put up its fees in 1891! Its achievements owed

*5   The 'original' college, Durning Road, Liverpool*

much to the work of Miss Yelf and her staff. Unfortunately Miss Yelf's health was not good and she was forced to retire in 1890 at the age of 44 (ironically she was to live to the age of 83!). The committee thanked her with a glowing testimonial:

> Miss Yelf by the wisdom with which she arranged the general rules, discipline and curriculum of the College, not less than by the conscientiousness, earnestness and christian temper of mind with which she addressed herself to the arduous duties of her anxious task soon raised the College to an honourable position among the Female Training Colleges of the kingdom, and she leaves it with the high rank of fifth on the list of all those Colleges as attested by the last Government examination. It is impossible for the Committee to speak too highly of the beneficient influence which Miss Yelf by her strength of character, firmness, loftiness of mind and affectionate solicitude for their truest welfare, has exercised upon the development of the characters of the Students committed to her charge.[4]

They decided to ask Dr. Fitch, the HMI, if he could recommend a suitable successor and at his suggestion Sarah J. Hale was offered the post. This decision was taken before the application of Miss Feuchsel, who had been acting principal, was even considered.[5] One can only infer that Miss Feuchsel was treated rather shabbily.

Miss Hale had begun her career as a pupil teacher, then became a student at Whitelands Training College. She had been headmistress of two elementary schools, at the first of which (a London slum school) she met and got on well with Matthew Arnold who was then an HMI. She soon moved to St Katharine's College, Tottenham where she was First Mistress. While at St Katharine's, she decided that she needed more academic training to do full justice to the job. She therefore resigned and went to Newnham College Cambridge where she took a third in Mental and Moral Science. Her next appointment was at Cheltenham Training College where she was Method Mistress. She had had a reasonable amount of experience prior to coming to Edge Hill, though it would seem that whom she knew counted for a great deal.

# 2
# MISS HALE'S PRINCIPALSHIP

**6**  *Miss Hale*

## I College Development 1890-1906

The period of Miss Hale's principalship, 1890-1920, was for Edge Hill a time of consolidation rather than radical change. Nationally, the structure of teacher training underwent considerable alteration. The foundation of day training colleges in 1890 led to changes in the syllabus of residential colleges who were now also allowed to take up university work and give certain students a third year of training.

Initially college syllabuses had followed broadly the same lines as the Queen's Scholarship Examination though in more depth. Students therefore studied practical teaching, reading and recitation, arithmetic, music, grammar, literature, geography, history and, again in line with conventional thought, maths for boys and needlework for girls. The one addition to the college timetable was school management. It is evident that specialisation was not envisaged; the idea was to produce a *class* not a subject teacher.

Geography, history and domestic economy were now to be optional in the second year and science or language could be studied instead of, or in addition to, the ordinary subjects in the curriculum. The examination for drawing was also changed. Students now received either a *First*

7   *The art room*

or *Second* Class Drawing Certificate according to their abilities in freehand, model, light and shade and geometrical drawing. Blackboard drawing was no longer compulsory. As far as Edge Hill itself was concerned, certain changes had also taken place: botany had been studied since 1891, mechanics was started in 1892 and physiography, maths and physics were added in 1893.

Another innovation of the Board of Education—day students—was not welcomed by Edge Hill. Five students were reluctantly admitted at the beginning of 1892. Their homes had to be within a convenient distance of the institution and they attended Edge Hill from 8.00 a.m. to 8.00 p.m., taking part in the entire work of the resident students, the only difference being that they had to sleep at home. (Whether these early day students were fully integrated into Edge Hill life is impossible to say. No attempt was made to adjust the routine to day students. Later generations certainly did not feel part of the community. Catherine Campbell [1932-4] recalled, 'We were never really accepted by the rest of the College and our only "home" was a cloakroom which we called "Clint" [Clint Road being adjacent]. We were rather like displaced persons'. Day students ceased with the move to Ormskirk in 1933 when Edge Hill became fully residential.)

A similar somewhat isolated group was the third-year university students. From 1894 students of sufficient calibre were able to read for university degrees. Originally students were prepared for London matriculation, classes were thus started for the Victoria Preliminary which led to affiliation to Victoria University (Manchester). They then moved to Liverpool where Edge Hill lecturers were recognised as teachers of the University so that students could spend their first year at Edge Hill. After three years they received a degree plus a professional certificate from the Board of Education. Edge Hill was very proud of the fact that 'of all the women's colleges, [it] has hitherto prepared the largest proportion of its students for degree courses'.[1] This proved an aid to recruitment: Ethel M. Ryley (student 1919-21) 'chose Edge Hill because,

8    Group of third year students, 1907

9    Third year students, 1912-13

along with Homerton, they were the only two colleges which combined teacher training and a degree course'. The practice of a non-university sector playing a role in degree teaching therefore has long antecedents.

Edge Hill's success in dealing with these developments can be judged by the HMI reports. Gradually a position of strength was being established. In 1895 it was described in glowing terms as almost the equivalent of a 19th-century holiday camp:

> Every care is taken to provide for the physical well-being, the intellectual development, and the efficient professional training of the students. The arrangements for securing these ends are made on a most liberal scale. The dietary is good and varied, there is a well-stocked library, the rooms are furnished with comfort and taste, and the surroundings of the students are calculated to refine their mind and manners.

(The emphasis on refinement once again suggests the wish to attract a more middle-class student.) The staff were strong in number and qualifications and the prospects of the institution 'bright and hopeful'. This promise was fulfilled, for by 1901 the HMI wrote, 'This is one of our most successful Colleges; 75% of the second years had "double firsts" in the Class List'. From then on the praise was constant; an example form 1902 is typical:

> This College more than maintains its reputation for thorough and intelligent work. A high ideal is aimed at. The tone of the students is excellent. They are bright, contented and diligent. Their success in their examinations is remarkable. The influence of the Principal is felt throughout. The staff are able, loyal and devoted. The practical training is intelligently carried out and carefully supervised … The Committee deserves credit for what they have accomplished.[2]

The Committee was quick to try to remedy any deficiencies detected by the HMIs. A lack of adequate facilities for cooking instruction was noted in 1894, 'the accommodation is bad. A new and properly constructed and arranged kitchen should be added to the premises, with a workroom or laboratory'. By 1895 this had been rectified. 'The kitchen has been enlarged and greatly improved.' The sleeping accommodation in the older part of the house, criticised in 1886, was sufficiently improved to satisfy the HMI by 1887. On 10 September 1889 it was stated that more sitting room was needed for both students and governesses and that the institution as a whole required a better standard of 'decoration and ornamentation'. Within a month 50 writing tables and 50 armchairs had been ordered and by February 1890 a scheme had been proposed to erect a new wing with a day room on the ground floor and accommodation for 13 on the first floor. The extra space would release room which could be used to give the governesses a sitting room. The cost was to be £2,000. By 9 September 1890 this work was in progress and completed and opened on 30 September 1891. An even quicker response came in October 1890; Fitch, the HMI, suggested that an additional governess should be appointed to teach drawing. Within *four days* it had been agreed to appoint one.

Accommodation, however, was to prove a continuing problem and one which was only solved briefly for a six-year period between 1933 and 1939. Edge Hill was further enlarged in 1893 by the renting of two houses adjoining it. This brought the total number of students up to 110 but was by no means a long-term solution. Plans were therefore drawn up for a new extension and appeals once again made for subscriptions. The work soon disrupted the everyday running of the institution, everything took place against a background of 'workmen's hammers— to say nothing of their whistling'. Even when the autumn term began in 1903 the workmen were still on the premises.

**10** *The north wing*

**11** *The entrance*

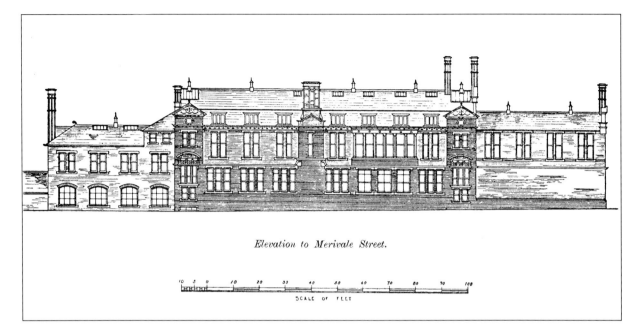

*Elevation to Merivale Street.*

SCALE OF FEET

**12**  *Proposed enlargement, 1901*

The two armies encamped on the same ground for weeks, in fact it was often a case of Box and Cox, for by night the students occupied dormitories, in which by day the carpenters were at work; some members of the staff corrected contentedly with a French polisher in one corner and an electrician in another; and lectures in the senior class-room were given to the tune of the putting up of a gallery in the room on the other side of the partition, and the fixing of hot water pipes in the corridor alongside. A convenient deafness to extraneous noises was cultivated, though at times those at the back of the classroom rose swiftly and deposited themselves and their note-books on the platform at the lecturer's feet, with a mute protest in their eyes, while the skilful speaker dodged the blows of the hammer, or spoke *via* the blackboard where possible.

Nevertheless both sides got on well and the new wing was opened on 31 October 1903 by the Marquis of Londonderry, Lord President of the Council and President of the Board of Education. It consisted of three new classrooms, two laboratories, a library and a gymnasium. Despite two additional dormitories, some students still had to sleep out. Edge Hill, however, could now take 160 students.

One problem remained: all the cost had not been subscribed and on 4, 5, 6 October 1906 a Bazaar was held in St George's Hall, Liverpool to raise funds to cover the debt of £7,000. Each day there was an opening ceremony taken by the Countess of Derby, Mrs. W.W. Pilkington, and Lady Stanley. The band of the Yorkshire Hussars provided music. The event was a great success; £3,976 was raised of which £3,900 was used to reduce the debt.[3]

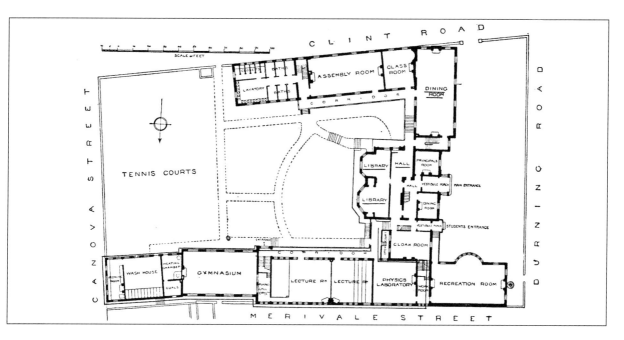

**13**  *Ground plan showing proposed enlargement, 1901*

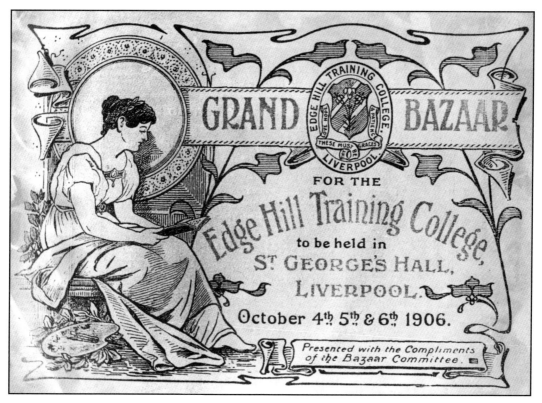

**14**  *The Grand Bazaar*

## II Development of Teacher Training 1902-1914

The period 1902-14 saw considerable changes in the regulations affecting training colleges. Prior to 1904 the Board of Education formulated training college syllabuses, prescribing a uniform curriculum for each subject. From 1904, however, colleges were given the freedom to draw up their own schemes providing these fell within a general outline laid down and approved by the Board. Students were to be taught the subjects needed in a secondary school as it was felt that these were also relevant to the primary. In practice this meant a great increase in the number of subjects. The second-year student had to take English language, literature and composition, history and geography, elementary mathematics, elementary science, hygiene, theory of music, principles of teaching, reading and repetition, drawing, needlework, singing and physical training. The state therefore was abandoning its attempt to direct every aspect of a teacher's education. Miss Hale commented, 'We are optimistic and therefore see in these Regulations possibilities that make for development and progress …'.[4]

She was not so pleased about the replacement from 1907 of the King's Scholarship entrance examination by the Preliminary Examination for the Certificate. The new examination was to be in two parts: Part One, composition and arithmetic; Part Two, English history, geography plus one option (elementary science, mathematics or a foreign language). Candidates were not graded into classes though distinctions were awarded to those passing any of the Part Two subjects with credit. Miss Hale was extremely scathing: she maintained that the tendencies of the 'Liberal' Government (her emphasis) were to lower standards for those teaching in elementary schools; to discourage working for a university degree during a training college course; and to separate completely primary and secondary schools. To enable as many as possible to enter training colleges, the standards of the Entrance Examination were to be lowered: the previous

*15   Garden side, south-east view*

year had seen those in the third class eligible, now there were to be no classes at all. This meant that colleges had little effective choice of candidates, 'the policy of "first come, first served" too often resulting in first come, and for all concerned *worst* served … It remains to be seen what the effect of this change will have on the future of the College.'[5] Such foreboding appeared to

*16    The library*

*17    The principal's room*

*18    Garden side, south view*

*19    The dining hall*

be justified. The students entering in 1907, 'as was anticipated' were 'widely differing in intellectual calibre and in attainments: the low position of many in the College List—classified on the results of the Examination at the end of the first year—shows that they are distinctly below the ordinary College standard'.[6]

**20**   *The lecture hall*

Another of Miss Hale's fears—that the increase in training colleges (there were to be an additional 11 by 1908 and places increased from 7,000 in 1903 to 12,000 in 1910) would lead to unemployment—also seemed to be well founded. The *Report* for 1907-8 revealed that 10 second-year students were still unemployed; by 1909 the situation had further deteriorated, 30 out of the 76 students leaving were without jobs. Miss Hale did not mince words: 'The question is a grave one, considering the encouragement given for the founding of new training colleges'. The 1902 Education Act had allowed 'the engagement of persons with very scanty qualifications'. She wished that the Board of Education would pressurise the Local Education Authorities to employ trained teachers and discourage the use of the untrained who were often preferred on grounds of economy. It was unfair to encourage people to train if jobs were not available. 'Much greater difficulty is anticipated in the near future, as the supply of trained people promises greatly to exceed the demand.'[7] In Lancashire only 800 out of 5,000, i.e. 16 per cent, were trained and certificated, yet among the unemployed 23 per cent of men and 32 per cent of women were trained teachers. This meant that *c.*£200,000 spent by the Exchequer in training them was giving no return. The oversupply of qualified teachers would lead to lower salaries which in turn would mean lower status and eventually lower qualifications.[8] No real improvement had occurred by 1910 when 21 out of 67 did not secure employment. Thereafter it began to level out and the War of course ensured that there was no shortage of positions.

The lowering of standards meant that some students found it increasingly difficult to cope with the large number of subjects which had to be studied. A change in regulations in 1913, which reduced the number to be taken and gave more time to professional studies, was therefore welcome. Subjects were grouped into three classes: professional (compulsory)—principles and practice of teaching; hygiene, physical training, theory of music and singing, reading and recitation, drawing, needlework; General Studies—students chose three or in special cases two from the following—English, history and geography, maths, elementary science; Additional subjects—

**21**   *The common room*

these were taken by those aiming to improve their general education—French, German, Latin, physics, chemistry, botany, rural science and housecraft.

Miss Hale thoroughly approved, since the object of the changes was to give more time to professional training—always an Edge Hill goal: '… the modified conditions will make it much easier for students who are weak or very inexperienced in teaching … seeing that they need not take up more than two or three subjects for the written examination in addition to the "professional" subjects'.[9]

## III  Patterns of Student Recruitment: Origins and Destinations

Despite the wishes of the founders that Edge Hill should cater for the needs of non-Anglicans, the institution did attract a significant number of Anglican students. Table I demonstrates that only in 1893 did the percentage fall below 37 per cent while in 10 of the years between 1887 and 1920 Anglicans formed over 50 per cent of the student intake. Edge Hill therefore was responding to a need for *teacher* training rather than merely a demand for non-denominational education. Indeed the Lord Mayor, when opening the new wing on 21 October 1903, maintained:

> It was very satisfactory to know that whilst the college was unsectarian the majority of the teachers trained there belonged to the Church of England, a condition which could not but give cause for thankfulness to members of that body.[10]

## TABLE I – Religion

| Year | Total | Church of England | | Non-conformist | |
|---|---|---|---|---|---|
| | | Number | % | Number | % |
| 1887 | 41 | 22 | 54 | 19 | 46 |
| 1888 | 39 | 18 | 46 | 21 | 54 |
| 1889 | 40* | 18 | 45 | 20 | 50 |
| 1890 | 39 | 22 | 56 | 17 | 44 |
| 1891 | 41* | 15 | 37 | 24 | 63 |
| 1892 | 47 | 27 | 57 | 20 | 43 |
| 1893 | 53 | 16 | 30 | 37 | 70 |
| 1894 | 55 | 21 | 38 | 34 | 62 |
| 1895 (Jan) | 56 | 22 | 39 | 34 | 61 |
| 1895 (Summer) | 53 | 26 | 49 | 27 | 51 |
| 1896 | 53 | 22 | 42 | 31 | 58 |
| 1897 | 55 | 25 | 45 | 30 | 55 |
| 1898 | 57 | 26 | 46 | 31 | 54 |
| 1899 | 53 | 23 | 43 | 30 | 57 |
| 1900 | 62 | 29 | 47 | 33 | 53 |
| 1901 | 62 | 27 | 44 | 35 | 56 |
| 1902 | 57 | 30 | 53 | 27 | 47 |
| 1903 | 68 | 25 | 37 | 43 | 63 |
| 1904 | 67 | 31 | 46 | 36 | 54 |
| 1905 | 68 | 31 | 46 | 37 | 54 |
| 1906 | 75 | 31 | 41 | 44 | 59 |
| 1907 | | | | | |
| 1908 | 72 | 32 | 44 | 40 | 56 |
| 1909 | 75 | 39 | 52 | 36 | 48 |
| 1910 | 68 | 30 | 44 | 38 | 56 |
| 1911 | 75 | 31 | 41 | 44 | 59 |
| 1912 | 65 | 31 | 48 | 34 | 52 |
| 1913 | 76 | 41 | 54 | 35 | 46 |
| 1914 | 70 | 31 | 44 | 39 | 56 |
| 1915 | 78 | 37 | 47 | 41 | 53 |
| 1916 | 72 | 42 | 58 | 30 | 42 |
| 1917 | 77 | 40 | 51 | 37 | 49 |
| 1918 | 71 | 39 | 55 | 32 | 45 |
| 1919 | 83 | 54 | 65 | 29 | 35 |
| 1920 | 67 | 30 | 45 | 37 | 55 |

\* Includes two whose religion was unknown.

The typical student was aged between 19 and 21 and had, till 1907, been a pupil teacher. In 1907 the bursary system was introduced whereby prospective students received a grant to encourage them to stay on at school till they were 17 or 18. They could then have a year as a student teacher before they trained. The popularity of this change is evident in the decline of the number of pupil teachers who became Edge Hill students and the predominance of the student teacher:

## TABLE II

| Date | No. of students | Pupil Teachers | Student Teachers | Unqualified Assistants | Bursars | Not Apprenticed |
|------|------|------|------|------|------|------|
| 1887 | 41 | 41 | | | | |
| 1888 | 39 | 38 | | | | 1 |
| 1889 | 40 | 39 | | | | 1 |
| 1890 | 39 | 39 | | | | |
| 1891 | 41 | 39 | | | | 2 |
| 1892 | 47 | 47 | | | | |
| 1893 | 53 | 52 | | | | 1 |
| 1894 | 55 | 55 | | | | |
| 1895-6 | 56 | 53 | | | | 3 |
| 1895-6-7 | 53 | 53 | | | | |
| 1896-7-8 | 53 | 53 | | | | |
| 1897-8-9 | 57 | 57 | | | | |
| 1898 | 55 | 55 | | | | |
| 1899 | 52 | 52 | | | | |
| | | | | | | |
| 1909 | 75 | 27 | 37 | 2 | 6 | 3 |
| 1910 | 68 | 13 | 49 | 2 | 3 | 1 |
| 1911 | 75 | 16 | 57 | 1 | 0 | 1 |
| 1912 | 65 | 8 | 56 | 0 | 0 | 1 |
| 1913 | 76 | 9 | 65 | 0 | 0 | 2 |
| 1914 | 70 | 5 | 62 | 1 | 2 | 0 |
| 1915 | 78 | 4 | 68 | 6 | 0 | 0 |
| 1916 | 72 | 3 | 67 | 2 | 0 | 0 |
| 1917 | 77 | 1 | 76 | 0 | 0 | 0 |
| 1918 | 71 | 5 | 65 | 1 | 0 | 0 |
| 1919 | 83 | 7 | 71 | 5 | 0 | 0 |
| 1920 | 67 | 1 | 61 | 4 | 1 | 0 |

Edge Hill therefore followed the national trend in urban areas of accepting the bursar/student teacher system.

Nor did it appear to have any difficulty in attracting the academically able; the average number on the scholarship list was high. In contrast to University College Cardiff, where the average position of men entrants on the scholarship list in 1892 was 1,092 and the most favourable for its first decade was 385,[11] Edge Hill students regularly surpassed this:

## TABLE III
### Scholarship List Number

| | |
|---|---|
| 1891 | All passed in the first class |
| 1893 | 386 |
| 1894 | 332 |
| 1895 (Jan) | 270 |
| 1895 (Summer) | 372 |
| 1896 | 344 |
| 1897 | 688 |
| 1898 | 388 |
| 1899-1900 | 741 |
| 1901-2 | 600 |
| 1902-3 | 510 |

It was always made quite clear, however, that intellectual ability was not the only or even main quality required in a prospective teacher:

> Alertness, pleasantness of manner, responsiveness, some amount of individuality, a real desire for the work—these are the characteristics which with a suitable home environment make themselves fairly evident. No lethargic, stolid, unobservant, unattractive—whether in speech or manner—or unsympathetic person, however physically strong, mentally well-equipped, and even morally sound should be accepted for the teaching profession … there should be no hesitancy on the part of the authorities in rejecting any who show lack of teaching aptitude.[12]

There is no doubt that Miss Hale and her staff had a clear idea of what qualities women teachers should have and these were supported by visiting dignatories. Dr. Watson, at the address to outgoing students in 1903, stated that the country was at a critical stage in its history, no longer enjoying the advantages of steam and commerce. His advice was heavily gendered: 'To men, … make the children keen and quick witted; to women, raise up women to create homes for the men and thereby great service to our country and fulfil the trust committed to us'.[13]

Education was evidently seen as a means of social control. At the 25th anniversary celebrations the bishop of the diocese endorsed this view to much applause:

**22**  *Twenty-fifth anniversary, 1910*

After 27 years of absence he came back to Lancashire, and he saw in more ways than one the effect of the teaching of the elementary schools in the refinement and the increased civility of the people of Lancashire (Applause). In these earlier days one never heard the word "sir", and never received anything more than a nod at the most and sometimes not that. But when ten years ago he came to Liverpool he was immensely struck by the courtesy of the great masses of the people, and he felt sure that that increase of courtesy and good manners was due very largely to the work of the teachers in the elementary schools (Applause).[14]

Edge Hill was designed to be a national rather than a local institution: 'to work it efficiently and economically it must receive a much larger number of students than the number which will be supplied from this neighbourhood'.[15] In terms of origin, however, students came overwhelmingly from Lancashire in general and Liverpool in particular (Tables IV, V). Only in 1905 and 1906 did Lancashire's percentage fall below 50 per cent and, except in 1905, Liverpool itself always contributed more than 20 per cent. Yorkshire sent the next largest contingent, though this fluctuated from 0 to 29 per cent. Apart from 1893 and 1902, 80 per cent plus of all students came from the neighbouring counties of Lancashire, Yorkshire, Cheshire and Cumberland. Edge Hill was essentially an institution of the north-west; less than 10 per cent came from outside this narrow catchment area.

## TABLE IV
### Origins

| Year | Lancs/L'pool | Yorkshire | Cheshire | Cumberland | Isle of Man | Wales | Staffordshire | Nottinghamshire | London | Derbyshire | Norfolk | Northamptonshire | Bristol | Warwick | Devon | Westmorland | Shropshire | Bedfordshire | Tyneside | Lincolnshire | Leicester | Cambridgeshire | Ireland | Sussex | Unknown |
|---|---|---|---|---|---|---|---|---|---|---|---|---|---|---|---|---|---|---|---|---|---|---|---|---|---|
| 1887 (41) | 32/19 | 1 | 2 |  | 2 | 2 | 1 | 1 |  |  |  |  |  |  |  |  |  |  |  |  |  |  |  |  |  |
| 1888 (39) | 32/20 |  | 2 |  |  | 2 | 1 |  | 1 |  |  |  |  |  |  |  |  |  |  |  |  |  |  |  | 1 |
| 1889 (40) | 30/15 | 3 | 1 |  | 1 |  |  |  | 3 | 1 |  |  |  |  |  |  |  |  |  |  |  |  |  |  | 1 |
| 1890 (39) | 33/24 |  | 2 |  |  | 1 |  |  | 3 |  | 1 |  |  |  |  |  |  |  |  |  |  |  |  |  |  |
| 1891 (41) | 26/15 | 5 | 2 |  |  | 1 |  |  | 3 | 2 |  |  |  |  |  |  |  |  |  |  |  |  |  |  | 1 |
| 1892 (47) | 37/29 | 3 | 2 |  |  | 1 |  |  | 3 |  |  |  |  |  |  |  |  |  |  |  |  |  |  |  | 1 |
| 1893 (53) | 32/19 | 7 |  |  | 1 | 3 | 2 |  | 6 |  |  | 1 |  |  |  |  |  |  |  |  |  |  |  |  | 1 |
| 1894 (55) | 31/17 | 11 | 2 | 1 |  |  | 5 |  | 4 |  |  |  |  |  |  |  |  |  |  |  |  |  |  |  | 1 |
| 1895 (56) | 37/18 | 8 |  | 1 |  | 1 | 1 |  | 4 | 1 |  |  |  |  |  |  |  |  |  |  |  |  |  |  | 3 |
| 1896 (53) | 36/19 | 13 |  |  |  |  |  |  | 1 |  |  |  |  | 1 | 1 |  |  |  |  |  |  |  |  |  | 1 |
| 1897 (55) | 34/22 | 15 | 4 |  |  |  |  |  |  |  |  |  |  | 2 |  |  |  |  |  |  |  |  |  |  |  |
| 1898 |  |  |  |  |  |  |  |  |  |  |  |  |  |  |  |  |  |  |  |  |  |  |  |  |  |
| 1899 (52) | 36/23 | 8 | 1 | 1 | 1 | 1 | 1 |  | 1 | 1 |  |  |  |  |  |  |  |  |  |  |  | 1 |  |  |  |
| 1900 |  |  |  |  |  |  |  |  |  |  |  |  |  |  |  |  |  |  |  |  |  |  |  |  |  |
| 1901 |  |  |  |  |  |  |  |  |  |  |  |  |  |  |  |  |  |  |  |  |  |  |  |  |  |
| 1902 (62) | 34/19 | 9 | 2 | 1 | 2 |  | 1 |  | 3 | 1 |  |  |  | 6 |  |  |  |  |  |  |  |  |  |  | 3 |
| 1903 |  |  |  |  |  |  |  |  |  |  |  |  |  |  |  |  |  |  |  |  |  |  |  |  |  |
| 1904 |  |  |  |  |  |  |  |  |  |  |  |  |  |  |  |  |  |  |  |  |  |  |  |  |  |
| 1905 (67) | 32/10 | 16 | 8 | 4 |  | 1 | 1 |  | 2 | 1 |  |  | 1 | 2 |  |  |  |  |  |  |  |  |  |  |  |
| 1906 (69) | 32/15 | 19 | 6 | 3 | 2 | 1 |  |  | 1 | 1 |  |  | 1 |  |  |  |  |  |  |  | 2 |  |  |  | 1 |
| 1907 (75) | 41/26 | 18 | 7 | 5 |  | 2 | 1 |  | 1 |  |  |  |  |  |  |  |  |  |  |  |  |  | 1 |  |  |
| 1908 (72) | 46/20 | 15 | 6 | 3 |  | 1 |  |  |  |  |  |  |  | 4 |  |  |  |  |  |  |  |  |  |  |  |
| 1909 (75) | 42/23 | 22 | 6 |  | 1 |  |  |  |  | 1 |  |  |  | 1 |  |  |  |  |  |  |  | 1 | 1 |  |  |
| 1910 (68) | 44/19 | 14 | 5 | 2 |  |  |  |  |  | 2 |  |  |  |  |  |  | 1 |  |  |  |  |  |  |  |  |
| 1911 (75) | 51/24 | 8 | 5 |  | 2 | 2 | 1 |  | 1 | 1 | 1 |  |  |  |  |  |  | 1 |  |  | 2 |  |  |  |  |
| 1912 (65) | 46/19 | 5 | 1 | 8 | 4 |  |  |  |  |  |  |  |  |  |  | 1 |  |  |  |  |  |  |  |  |  |
| 1913 (76) | 60/20 | 11 | 1 |  | 2 |  |  |  |  |  |  |  |  |  |  |  |  |  | 1 | 1 |  |  |  |  |  |
| 1914 (70) | 50/20 | 7 | 4 | 2 | 3 | 1 |  |  |  | 1 |  |  |  |  |  |  |  |  |  | 1 | 1 |  |  |  |  |
| 1915 (78) | 44/16 | 9 | 9 | 3 | 6 |  | 2 | 1 |  |  |  | 1 |  | 1 |  |  | 1 |  |  | 1 |  |  |  |  |  |
| 1916 (72) | 59/25 | 6 | 1 | 1 | 1 |  | 2 |  |  |  |  |  |  |  |  |  |  |  | 1 | 1 |  |  |  |  |  |
| 1917 (77) | 57/22 | 5 | 9 | 3 | 1 |  |  |  |  |  |  |  |  | 2 |  |  |  |  |  |  |  |  |  |  |  |
| 1918 (71) | 43/15 | 15 | 7 | 3 | 3 |  |  |  |  |  |  |  |  |  |  |  |  |  |  |  |  |  |  |  |  |

## TABLE V
## Origins %

|  | Lancs/ Liverpool | Yorkshire | Cumberland Cheshire |  | Total |
|---|---|---|---|---|---|
| 1887 (41) | 78/46 | 2 | 5 | 0 | 85 |
| 1888 (39) | 82/51 | 0 | 5 | 0 | 87 |
| 1889 (40) | 75/38 | 7 | 3 | 0 | 85 |
| 1890 (39) | 85/62 | 0 | 5 | 0 | 90 |
| 1891 (41) | 63/37 | 12 | 5 | 0 | 80 |
| 1892 (47) | 78/62 | 6 | 4 | 0 | 88 |
| 1893 (53) | 60/36 | 13 | 0 | 0 | 73 |
| 1894 (55) | 56/31 | 20 | 4 | 2 | 82 |
| 1895 (56) | 66/32 | 14 | 0 | 2 | 82 |
| 1896 (53) | 68/36 | 25 | 0 | 0 | 83 |
| 1897 (55) | 62/40 | 27 | 7 | 0 | 96 |
| 1898 |  |  |  |  |  |
| 1899 (52) | 69/44 | 15 | 2 | 2 | 88 |
| 1900 |  |  |  |  |  |
| 1901 |  |  |  |  |  |
| 1902 (62) | 58/31 | 15 | 3 | 2 | 78 |
| 1903 |  |  |  |  |  |
| 1904 |  |  |  |  |  |
| 1905 (67) | 48/15 | 24 | 12 | 6 | 80 |
| 1906 (69) | 46/22 | 28 | 9 | 4 | 87 |
| 1907 (75) | 55/35 | 24 | 9 | 7 | 95 |
| 1908 (72) | 64/28 | 21 | 8 | 4 | 97 |
| 1909 (75) | 56/31 | 29 | 8 | 0 | 92 |
| 1910 (68) | 65/28 | 21 | 7 | 3 | 96 |
| 1911 (75) | 68/32 | 11 | 7 | 0 | 86 |
| 1912 (65) | 71/29 | 8 | 2 | 12 | 93 |
| 1913 (76) | 79/26 | 14 | 1 | 0 | 94 |
| 1914 (70) | 71/29 | 10 | 6 | 3 | 90 |
| 1915 (78) | 56/21 | 12 | 12 | 4 | 84 |
| 1916 (72) | 82/35 | 8 | 1 | 1 | 92 |
| 1917 (77) | 74/29 | 6 | 12 | 4 | 96 |
| 1918 (71) | 61/21 | 21 | 10 | 4 | 96 |

A similar pattern is observed when it came to the destinations of those leaving Edge Hill: except for 1897 and 1911, Lancashire and Yorkshire together took over 70 per cent of the certificated students with Liverpool itself usually securing over 20 per cent (Tables VI, VII). Loyalty to one's home area was even stronger: more than 50 per cent usually returned to the same town and a number even to the same school (Table VIII), while of the remainder many moved within the same county, e.g. Bradford to Leeds. This was in line with established practice:

the *Board of Education Report* for 1912-13 commented, ' … many students, especially women students, desire to obtain posts in or near their homes, and hesitate to accept appointments in some unfamiliar or distant parts of the country'.[16] Even unemployment did not force students to move. Miss Hale disapproved strongly: 'It is regretted that seven have felt obliged to accept appointment as uncertificated teachers rather than go out of Liverpool'.[17] Edge Hill then was not a national institution, nor did its students use it as a means of mobility, of escaping parental control.[18]

## TABLE VI
## Destination

| Year | (n) | Lancs/L'pool | Yorkshire | Cheshire | Cumberland | Isle of Man | Wales | Staffordshire | Nottinghamshire | London | Derbyshire | Norfolk | Northamptonshire | Bristol | Warwick | Devon | Westmorland | Durham | Shropshire | Bedfordshire | Tyneside | Lincolnshire | Leicester | Middlesex | Oxford | Scotland | Kent | Sunderland |
|---|---|---|---|---|---|---|---|---|---|---|---|---|---|---|---|---|---|---|---|---|---|---|---|---|---|---|---|---|
| 1891 | (38) | 20/15 | 9 | 2 | | | | | | 4 | | | | | | | | | | | | | | | | | | |
| 1892 | | | | | | | | | | | | | | | | | | | | | | | | | | | | |
| 1893 | | | | | | | | | | | | | | | | | | | | | | | | | | | | |
| 1894 | (55) | 25/15 | 15 | | 1 | 1 | 1 | | | 8 | 1 | | | | 1 | | | | | | | | | | 2 | | | |
| 1895 | (52) | 27/16 | 13 | 2 | 1 | | 1 | | | 2 | 3 | 1 | | | 1 | | | | | | 1 | | | | | | | |
| 1896 | (48) | 28/12 | 9 | 2 | | | 1 | | | 4 | 1 | | | | 1 | | | | | | | | | | | 1 | 1 | |
| 1897 | (50) | 25/16 | 8 | 4 | | 2 | 1 | 4 | | 5 | | | | | 1 | | | | | | | | | | | | | |
| 1898 | (50) | 33/16 | 10 | 1 | | | | | | 1 | | | | | 4 | | | | | | 1 | | | | | | | |
| 1899 | | | | | | | | | | | | | | | | | | | | | | | | | | | | |
| 1900 | (49) | 27/8 | 17 | | 1 | | | | | 1 | | | | | 2 | | | | | | | 1 | | | | | | |
| 1901 | | | | | | | | | | | | | | | | | | | | | | | | | | | | |
| 1902 | (47) | 25/13 | 11 | 5 | | | | | | | | | | | 5 | | | | 1 | | | | | | | | | |
| 1903 | (27) | 15/7 | 6 | 3 | 1 | 1 | | | | | | | | | 1 | | | | | | | | | | | | | |
| 1904 | (40) | 28/16 | 6 | 3 | | | 1 | | | | | | | | 2 | | | | | | | | | | | | | |
| 1905 | (40) | 23/10 | 8 | 2 | 1 | | | | 3 | | | | | | 2 | | | | 1 | | | | | | | | | |
| 1906 | (53) | 29/22 | 16 | 2 | | | | | 3 | | | | | | 1 | | | | 2 | | | | | | | | | |
| 1907 | (46) | 28/9 | 8 | 7 | | 1 | | | | | 1 | | | | 1 | | | | 1 | | | | | | | | | |
| 1908 | (45) | 27/10 | 13 | 5 | | | | | | | | | | | | | | | | | | | | | | | | |
| 1909 | (46) | 22/10 | 11 | 8 | | 1 | 1 | | | | | | | | 1 | | | 2 | | | | | | | | | | |
| 1910 | (30) | 14/4 | 9 | 2 | | | | | | | | | | | 5 | | | | | | | | | | | | | |
| 1911 | (48) | 22/5 | 11 | 5 | | | 1 | | 3 | | | | | | | | | 3 | | | | | | | | | 1 | 2 |
| 1912 | (46) | 22/11 | 6 | 5 | | | 1 | | 4 | | | | | | | | | 7 | | | | 1 | | | | | | |
| 1913 | | | | | | | | | | | | | | | | | | | | | | | | | | | | |
| 1914 | (48) | 36/17 | 7 | 1 | 2 | | | | 1 | | | | | | 1 | | | | | | | | | | | | | |
| 1915 | (60) | 41/9 | 12 | 3 | | | | | | | | | | | 3 | | | 1 | | | | | | | | | | |
| 1916 | (57) | 42/15 | 5 | 7 | 1 | | | | | | | | | | 1 | | | | | | | | | 1 | | | | |
| 1917 | (60) | 37/16 | 8 | 10 | 1 | 1 | | 2 | | | | | | | | | | | | | 1 | | | | | | |
| 1918 | (63) | 49/25 | 3 | 3 | | | | 2 | | 1 | | | | | 4 | | | 1 | | | | | | | | | | |
| 1919 | (71) | 51/21 | 5 | 9 | 1 | 1 | | | | | | | | | 2 | | | 2 | | | | | | | | | | |

**TABLE VII**
**Destination %**

| | Lancs/ Liverpool | Yorkshire | Cumberland Cheshire | | Total |
|---|---|---|---|---|---|
| 1891 (38) | 53/39 | 24 | 5 | 0 | 82 |
| 1892 | | | | | |
| 1893 | | | | | |
| 1894 (55) | 45/27 | 27 | 0 | 0 | 72 |
| 1895 (52) | 52/31 | 25 | 4 | 2 | 83 |
| 1896 (48) | 58/25 | 19 | 4 | 0 | 81 |
| 1897 (50) | 50/32 | 16 | 8 | 0 | 74 |
| 1898 (50) | 66/32 | 20 | 2 | 0 | 88 |
| 1899 | | | | | |
| 1900 (49) | 55/16 | 35 | 0 | 0 | 90 |
| 1901 | | | | | |
| 1902 (47) | 53/28 | 23 | 11 | 0 | 87 |
| 1903 (27) | 56/26 | 22 | 11 | 4 | 93 |
| 1904 (40) | 70/40 | 15 | 8 | 0 | 93 |
| 1905 (40) | 58/25 | 20 | 5 | 3 | 86 |
| 1906 (53) | 55/42 | 30 | 4 | 0 | 89 |
| 1907 (46) | 61/20 | 17 | 15 | 0 | 93 |
| 1908 (45) | 60/22 | 29 | 11 | 0 | 90 |
| 1909 (46) | 48/22 | 24 | 17 | 0 | 89 |
| 1910 (30) | 47/13 | 30 | 7 | 0 | 34 |
| 1911 (48) | 46/10 | 23 | 10 | 0 | 79 |
| 1912 (46) | 48/24 | 13 | 11 | 0 | 72 |
| 1913 | | | | | |
| 1914 (48) | 75/35 | 15 | 2 | 4 | 96 |
| 1915 (60) | 68/32 | 20 | 5 | 0 | 93 |
| 1916 (57) | 74/26 | 9 | 12 | 2 | 97 |
| 1917 (60) | 62/27 | 13 | 17 | 2 | 94 |
| 1918 (63) | 78/40 | 5 | 5 | 0 | 88 |
| 1919 (71) | 72/30 | 7 | 13 | 1 | 93 |

N.B. Total number of students for each year does not correlate with the number given for the same year in Tables IV, V 'Origins' since the students (1) graduated two years later; (2) not all completed the course while some took a third year; (3) not all secured employment.

**TABLE VIII**
**Destinations**
**Same Town/Same School**

| Year | Number | % |
|------|--------|---|
| 1888 (41) | 26/2 | 63/5 |
| 1889 (41) | 24/2 | 59/5 |
| 1890 (40) | 19/3 | 48/8 |
| 1891 (39) | 25/7 | 64/18 |
| 1892 (41) | 26/4 | 63/10 |
| 1893 (47) | 32/10 | 68/21 |
| 1894 (55) | 35/10 | 64/18 |
| 1895 (55) | 36/10 | 65/18 |
| 1896 (48) | 39/6 | 81/13 |
| 1897 (50) | 39/8 | 78/16 |
| | | |
| 1905 (40) | 31/8 | 78/20 |
| 1906 (51) | 39/10 | 76/20 |
| 1907 (48) | 33/2 | 69/4 |
| 1908 (45) * | 35/10 | 78/22 |
| 1909 (47) * | 30/4 | 48/6 |
| 1910 (33) * | 28/7 | 85/21 |
| 1911 (49) * | 23/4 | 47/8 |
| 1912 (48) * | 22/1 | 49/2 |

* Total number of students does not include the unemployed, 1908–12

A slightly different picture emerges when the graduates are considered. Here the definite trend was to move, sometimes relatively long distances, e.g. from Blackburn to Horsham (West Sussex). By 1907 there had been 96 graduates—66 BA and 30 BSc. Lancashire employed less than half of these (in contrast to the non-graduates) and Lancashire, Cheshire and Yorkshire together took 69 per cent. As might be expected, the more academic graduates did tend to secure rather more prestigious jobs though this was not a uniform trend: in some years the type of employment acquired was very similar to that of the non-graduates. Analysis of the 96 graduates reveals that only 12 had become lecturers (three were in post at Edge Hill), three were HMIs, three science mistresses, one first assistant and the vast majority (72) were assistant teachers. Despite the large number of science graduates (30), only three had jobs as science mistresses. Nor did the passage of time alter the position much: by 1920 only 41 of the original group were still in employment. The number of lecturers had diminished to three, HMIs to two, science mistresses had doubled to six, first assistants to two and one had become a local inspector, the majority (27) were still assistants.

## TABLE IX
### Destinations of Graduates by 1907

| Total 96 | Lancs/ Liverpool | Yorks | Cheshire | Wales | Durham | Derbys. | Midlands | South |
|---|---|---|---|---|---|---|---|---|
| Number | 42/20 | 16 | 8 | 1 | 1 | 3 | 9 | 16 |
| % | 44/21 | 17 | 8 | 1 | 1 | 3 | 9 | 17 |

# IV Salaries

The initial staff were appointed at the following salaries: Miss Yelf £200 p.a.; First Governess, Miss Harriet Feuchsel at £90 with three increments of £10 to a maximum of £120; Second Governess, Miss Mildred Fenemore £70, by £10 increments to £90; Third Governess, Miss Dewhurst, £60 by £5 increments to £80.[19]

Eleven years later (1896) the staff consisted of the Principal, First Governess and five other resident governesses. The salary for the First Governess had improved quite considerably since she now started at £120, received increments of £5 for two years, then £10 for a further two years to a maximum of £150. The overall position of the other Governesses, however, had not changed, but in some respects had worsened since the level of increments was now lower:

> one starting at £70 by £5 increments to £90
> one starting at £65 by £5 increments to £80
> one starting at £60 by £5 increments to £90
> one starting at £60 by £5 increments to £80
> one starting at £55 by £5 increments to £80

Mrs. Evans, the housekeeper and cook, a trained teacher who taught cooking, started on £80 increasing by £5 increments to £100. The governesses were not allowed to do outside work and were to work an eight-hour day.

The salaries for the governesses do not appear over-generous and indeed, when Miss Fenemore resigned in 1886 to get married, the Committee wished to engage a replacement starting at £75 p.a. Miss Yelf, however, reported that she was finding difficulty in attracting anyone at that rate and the Committee agreed that £80 could be offered 'if necessary'. Miss Tucker was appointed at the higher figure.

The Principals fared better. Miss Yelf's salary was £200 p.a. When Miss Hale replaced her in 1890 she received £250 which by 1910 had been increased to £400 together with board and lodgings worth a further £85. Miss Cunnington was appointed as the first Vice-Principal in December 1905 at a salary of £120 and only held the position for six months before resigning in June 1906.[20] She was replaced by Miss J.A. Jenkins at a lower salary of £100 (this became standard Edge Hill practice: whenever someone left an attempt was always made to employ a cheaper replacement). This was increased from 1 September 1907 to £120 with two increments to a maximum of £150. Thereafter rises came quite regularly:

|  |  |
|---|---|
| 1909 | £160 |
| 1910 | £170 |
| 1912 | £200 |
| 1918 | £250 plus board and lodging worth £65. |

Over this period therefore her salary increased from approximately half that of the Principal to two-thirds. When acting Principal, however (October 1909—April 1910), she received only a bonus of 60 guineas (£63).[21]

A rudimentary system of salary scales was adopted though there appears no discernible reason for the way in which these were used. By 1909 the Finance Committee had some misgivings over the value of this: it was 'not advisable to apply the principle of automatic increases of Salaries from year to year, but rather that the increases of Salaries be a matter of consideration by the Committee from time to time'.[22] Those who were entitled to automatic increases were to continue to receive them until their maxima were reached, then it was up to the Committee. Accordingly many got nothing in 1909. Salaries were revised annually though not everyone benefited; the average increase was £5 but Miss Hale received a whopping £50 in 1910 while Miss Jenkins got only £10. In 1914 because of the financial state of the country no one was to get a rise except Miss Gowland who was awarded £10.[23]

From 1 September 1920 the Burnham scale was adopted, bringing a degree of uniformity. Miss Smith, who had started on £500 from 1 September 1920, immediately enjoyed £700, while her full salary in 1922 was reckoned to be £800. National scales were paid from then on. This meant that Miss Smith was receiving more in 1922 than the Professor of International Politics at Aberystwyth did in 1931!

## v  College Life

Students were subjected to a spartan regime designed to keep them busy all day: 'The routine was inflexible—we slept, ate worked and took walks, attended lectures and church and fulfilled extraneous duties from which no excuse could be contemplated'.[24] The day began (in 1890) at 6.15 a.m. when the rising bell was sounded. The fashions of the late 19th/early 20th centuries made dressing a lengthy business: since frocks had to be fastened down the back, for quickness the girls descended the stone staircase buttoning each other's clothes. Nor did all the lecturers find it easy to get up. Agnes Sutton (née Allcott), 1893-4, recalled, 'The governesses used to take a week in turn to be in charge, and we were highly amused when one of them, who shall be nameless, often slipped her dress over her night-dress, and slipped out to dress properly … before … breakfast was served!'. Prayers were said at 7 a.m., then there was class work till breakfast at 8 a.m. As soon as this was finished, students made their beds, dusted and tidied their rooms (two feather dusters 'Turkey' [a large one] and 'Chicken' [a small one] were provided) ready for inspection by the nurse. Apart from fetching and carrying their own washing water and certain dinner duties this was the only domestic work undertaken by the students. By contemporary standards it was considered light and perhaps again reflected Edge Hill's concern to attract a 'superior' type of girl. The HMI Fitch commented in 1888 and 1889 that he was glad that Edge Hill students had not so much household and laundry work as those in other colleges.

Nine o'clock to noon saw the seniors doing classwork while the juniors were engaged in school or study and cooking.

|             |                      |
|-------------|----------------------|
| 12.00-12.30 | was recreation       |
| 12.30       | dinner               |
| 2.30-4.30   | classwork (juniors)  |
|             | school or study (seniors) |

*23   College life*

A plain tea at 4.30 p.m. was followed by a walk between 5 p.m. and 6 p.m. Reflecting the more liberal conditions of the late century, this could be taken 'in any direction' and was not supervised by staff but at least two students had to go together. Then came a further two hours study (6-8 p.m.) with supper at 8.30 p.m., prayers at 9 p.m., and silence from 9.45 p.m. till lights out at 10 p.m. (this last period was designed to give an opportunity for private prayer). Students were responsible for seeing that all windows were shut before bedtime. If one was found open, a governess would wake up the person on window duty to make sure it was closed.

The day was long; the hours of study were 5¾ in class and 5½ either in the practising school, household work or private study. Students were split into two groups; each in turn received instruction morning and afternoon in class or did schoolwork, cookery, industrial work and private study. Four to six students were 'morning servers'; between 9 a.m. and 10 a.m. they cleared tables, washed cups, saucers and plates. They then studied till noon when they set the tables for dinner and waited. This was a particularly nerve-wracking experience for the new student: 'The unfortunate victims had to rush to the dining room, fight for a dozen knives, forks, spoons with which to set the table (always somebody was without the required number and appeals to the kitchen were ignored!)'.[25] Others helped prepare the meal, while a third set checked that the bathrooms were in order. Afternoon servers had to see that the tables were cleared and set for tea while afternoon cooks had 'easy duties' which lasted only till 3 p.m. and consisted 'mainly of the concocting of dainty dishes'. This may have been light by contemporary standards but it no doubt reinforced the value of the domestic ideology for the students.

To ensure that Edge Hill produced good practical teachers, the Committee arranged for an extra long period to be spent in the practising school.[26] Students taught 2½ hours daily for four days a week and stayed in one department for one month. They were supervised by head teachers and had to prepare lesson notes each week. Senior students were responsible (as far as practical) for some of the classes' subjects. Friday afternoons were devoted to 'criticism' sessions where a student gave a lesson criticised by the Principal, the head teacher, staff and fellow students. Given the emphasis on teaching practice it was rather ironic that the HMI's report of 1889 should state that 'teaching' was the only subject where the students were below average. Edge Hill was the only institution to provide more teaching practice than required by the Board (for which it was commended in 1892). There was, however, a certain disquiet about the heavy work-load: in 1894 the HMI commented, 'The time-table shows a heavy amount of

*24*   *The dining hall*

mental work, and a comparatively slight amount of time for private study and recreation'. And two years later (1896) he was still registering concern: 'Efforts will no doubt continue to be made to secure a substantial respite from study for every student in the course of the day, which is all the more important because the College does not possess very extensive grounds for the Physical exercise of so many young persons'. The emphasis throughout was on order and control. The governesses constantly supervised the girls during the working day; while it was the senior students' responsibility to enforce discipline during recreation times and special monitors were in charge of the dormitories. Students were not allowed to leave the premises after 5 p.m. between Monday and Friday. Saturday afternoons were free though permission was required to leave the institution. All had to be back by 7 p.m. (except in special circumstances). The rest of Saturday evening was spent doing needlework or drawing while the Principal read aloud from an 'interesting or instructive book'. Saturday evening lectures were introduced in the autumn of 1891. These were open to former students and friends and were of an improving nature. A far cry from today! Indeed as late as 1913-15 a governess was horrified to find that 'when she gave "extension" on Saturday night for students to go to the "Pictures" they had meant the Cinema and not the Art Gallery'.

Sundays were relatively free. After breakfast, Miss Hale gave a talk known as 'meditation'. This was not popular, as Norah Howie (1907-9) recalled: 'Most of it was above my head and to judge by faces around me, to many others too'. Each student was then supposed to attend the church of her denomination (though Edge Hill was undenominational students were required to attend daily, morning and evening prayers). A check was made at the 8 p.m. roll call when the girls had to answer 'once' or 'twice', signifying the number of times they had been at church. Those replying 'once' had to explain why to Miss Hale. Some used church as an opportunity to get out into the country. They travelled by tram to Wavertree and after 'a few minutes kneeling in the porch of a Roman Catholic Chapel, and possibly being sprinkled with Holy Water' went for a 'semi-rural' walk before returning to Edge Hill in time for dinner.

Every minute of the day therefore was strictly accounted for, and till 1889 students had no sitting room in which to relax (neither for that matter did the governesses). The HMI, Dr. Fitch, called attention to this in his report of that year and said that of the two, the students' need was the more important. He also called for better decoration and 'ornamentations'. The Committee's immediate response was to alter the Assembly Room and to install for the students 50 writing tables and 50 armchairs. In the longer term they planned an additional wing with a day room on the ground floor and sleeping accommodation for 13 on the first floor. This would release space which could then be used to give the governesses a lounge.

Accommodation therefore was very basic: all students were entitled to a cubicle (known as a 'cube') partitioned by wooden panels which ended about four to five feet from the ceiling. This gave very little privacy 'for every sound could be heard throughout the dormitory', though whether this was fundamentally different from conditions in an upper-class boarding school is difficult to determine.[27] Each cubicle contained a small chest of drawers, a little wash stand, a single bed (with a quilt known as a 'white elephant' which was turned down when friends visited because it had to be kept clean for a whole term), a desk and one or two shelves for books. There were no lights in the rooms, only one large one in the corridor which was turned off at 'lights out'; candles were not allowed. Hot water was also lacking: the wash stands boasted only a basin and a jug of cold water which had to be brought each morning from along the corridor. Here again strict restrictions were in force: students were not allowed to wash in their cubicles between 9 a.m. and 9 p.m. but had to use the general lavatory. Baths were taken according to a timetable; each student was allotted 15 minutes and to reach the bathroom had to walk down two corridors and a flight of stairs. (Even this however was a marked improvement to the situation in France, where at Sèvres—the establishment for educating teachers for the new lycées and colleges—baths were allowed only once every three weeks. Furthermore there was a Government enquiry to ensure that there was no unnecessary use of heating and lighting, as when the students were not in their rooms.)[28]

In the 1890s, Thursday nights at Edge Hill were a highlight because then the students went for an hour to a gym in Liverpool. Their clothes, however, were still extremely restrictive. They wore 'thick blue serge tunics buttoned up to the neck and with long sleeves, and "bloomers" … to match. Over this outfit, even in summer, we had to put on our dress skirts, for it was considered indecent to show even our ankles. What shapeless bundles of humanity we must have looked, and how hot we were in summer'. (Agnes Sutton, 1893-4.)

By 1904 Edge Hill had its own fully equipped gym, being the first institution to adopt the new Swedish system of gymnastics (an Edge Hill Certificate qualification gave exemption from the need for an LCC certificate) and gym kit now consisted of a navy blue dress with a red sailor collar. 'In these, the whole body was free to move as Nature intended, and the hems were a whole eleven inches from the ground!!.' Once the PT lesson was over, however, normal dress (voluminous skits with tightly boned corsets) was resumed.[29]

No doubt their experience of regulation and restriction during their time as pupil teachers helped many to adapt to and accept this controlled existence. Edna Walker (1915-17), writing in 1964, could not remember 'feeling rebellious at the restrictions'. Others, however, felt that 'the worst of the old system was that in 1904 we were treated as irresponsible beings, and subjected to excessive rules and restrictions'.[30]

**25**  *The gymnasium*

This certainly seems to have been the case; any attempts at real private study appear to have been actively discouraged. 'The most absurd rule I [K.W. Wild] can remember was that, though we each had a tiny private cubicle, we weren't allowed to use it for study. One of the jobs of the staff on duty was to go poking round and hustle off any ardent but erring reader. I was too frequently turned out of the very pleasant library' (K.W. Wild, 1907-10). Miss Wild took a first-class honours in Philosophy from London. This contrasted markedly with conditions for a university student of the same era who could enjoy her own study bedroom and the freedom to work whenever she wished. Restrictions did not end when the student left college. Headmistresses had almost despotic powers: one banned the reading of *Jane Eyre* by teachers unless they were aged at least twenty-five! Their authority extended even to the teacher's private life; one assistant in 1917 was reprimanded for smoking in her lodgings following a complaint by her landlady.[31]

Where 'open rebellion' occurred at Edge Hill it was over the food. Sample menus suggest that meals were reasonable:

| Sunday | Breakfast | Cold meat, bread and butter, tea and coffee |
|---|---|---|
| | Dinner | Roast pork, vegetables, rice pudding |
| | Tea | Bread and butter, tea, jam |
| | Supper | Biscuits, milk |
| Monday | Breakfast | Bacon, porridge, tea and coffee |
| | Dinner | Roast mutton and onion sauce, potatoes and cabbage |
| | Tea | Bread and butter, tea |
| | Supper | Bread and cheese, coffee and cocoa |
| Tuesday | For some reason nothing is given | |

26    *Gym practice*

27    *Gym certificate*

This is to Certify that

Miss *Winifred E. Wood*

has attended a Course of Instruction in the Theory and Practice of

SWEDISH GYMNASTICS

(FREE MOVEMENTS),

and that upon Examination she was placed in the *First* Class.

(Signed) *Florence L. Stansfeld.*

*Certificate, Hampstead Physical Training College.*

*J. A. Jenkins.* Vice-Principal.        *June 28th* 1909.

| Wednesday | Breakfast | Bacon, porridge, tea and coffee |
| | Dinner | Baked cod, vegetables, boiled bread pudding, fruit |
| | Tea | Bread and butter, tea |
| | Supper | Bread and butter, coffee and cocoa |
| Thursday | Breakfast | Fish, porridge, bread and butter, tea and coffee |
| | Dinner | Roast beef, vegetables |
| | Tea | Bread and butter, hot cakes, tea |
| | Supper | Cake or biscuits and milk |
| Friday | Breakfast | Cold meat, bread and butter, tea and coffee |
| | Dinner | Stewed rabbit and suet balls, vegetables |
| | Tea | Bread and butter, tea, jam |
| | Supper | Soup |
| Saturday | Breakfast | Bacon, bread and butter, tea and coffee |
| | Dinner | Steak pies, vegetables |
| | Tea | Bread and butter, marmalade, tea |
| | Supper | Bread and butter, coffee and cocoa |

K.W. Wild (1907-10) and Dorothy Waid (1904-6) made an interesting distinction that it was the cooking that was bad rather than the food itself:

> The menu for meals was quite good though not exciting. The cooking at one time was shocking … Wednesdays and Fridays were known as 'Psalm, Fish and Mystery' days because we sang psalms instead of hymns at Morning Prayer and at dinner we had what we called 'Mersey Whale' (a whole fish sent to table swimming in a sea of greasy water), and Mystery, a revolting sloppy mixture of flour, bread crumbs, dried fruit and huge lumps of suet. On Wednesdays also, one girl at each table of eleven girls would spend a shilling on cake or some seasonable dainty to add to the plain bread and butter provided for tea. Helena Normanton, later famous as one of the first women Barristers, was head girl when she was instructed by the Principal to ask us to forego our cake one Wednesday and give its cost to the Benevolent Fund … I was deputed to suggest that Helena should tell Miss Hale that we would rather give up our Wednesday dinner and have the cost of that given to the fund and retain our cake at tea time. Helena did so and Miss Hale was most annoyed that the complaint had not been made before. Henceforth the fish was cooked in an appetising way and very good fruit pudding was served.[32]

Such improvement, however, seemed temporary, for only a year later K.W. Wild recorded 'naked fish … in a sea of lukewarm water'. She pointed out that Edge Hill was only allowed 5p per head per day and relates that they had real butter and 'quite enough to eat … What was galling was that years later we were asked to subscribe for a present to the indifferent cooks. I didn't.'

The standard of cuisine can be gauged from the fact that little change can be detected in conditions during wartime. Added protein did, however, appear in the shape of cockroaches: 'the ovens in the kitchen were overrun with cockroaches, which were often to be found in our food, and our Parents were asked for money to provide new ovens'. (E.M. Ryley, 1919-21.)

Despite this, the health of the students was very good; the insistence on this in admission regulations seems to have paid off. The HMI reported in 1887 that it actually improved during their stay at Edge Hill, a position which was maintained with the result that the hospital was able to be used for a classroom and blackboard drawing room in 1895. Between 1885 and 1915 there were 61 deaths (0.1% p.a.) 'which compares very favourably with the general death rate, and shows that teaching is not an unhealthy profession'.[33]

## VI Student Societies

Participation in student societies was an important part of student life. Clubs for tennis, hockey, badminton, croquet and swimming enjoyed a full programme of activities while the Debating Society appeared to be *the* society in the sense that *all* students took part. The Christian Union also boasted 100 members in 1910 and undertook 'practical work' in that it provided treats for poor children having raised the money by general collections. Other flourishing societies included the 'Pons Asinorum' which appeared to be devoted to the study of literature (both prose and poetry); the French Society where 'members were invited to bring needlework, and finish each evening with games'; Music Societies and the Science Society. The Science Society was heavily academic: it was founded by the Third Year Science Students (i.e. the university students) and some of the 'Normal Class'. Average attendance was around twenty, 'as only those really interested in science are desired'.[35]

Edge Hill's student societies were important in providing a chance for relaxation, though, apart from the games clubs, this was still of a highly improving nature. It is interesting to note the number of times to which needlework is referred (members of the Pons Asinorum used

*28    The hockey team, 1911-12*

their meetings to make clothes for Liverpool poor children to have at Christmas). Students were not expected merely to be passive members of an audience but to be busying themselves with good works. In contrast to students at the University of Aberdeen it does not seem that the societies were dominated by a select few.[36] There was little or no overlap in office bearers in the different societies and membership numbers suggest that each student was a member of at least one society.

## VII  Politics and the Woman Question

There appear to have been no clubs devoted specifically to politics. The one instance of college-wide interest in politics came with a mock election in 1910 reflecting feelings in the country at large. Initially the three parties (Conservative, Liberal and Labour) were to stand but, as Labour only had three members, it joined the Liberals. Edge Hill as a whole attended the mass meetings and the result was Liberal 105 votes, Conservative 83, giving a Liberal majority of 22; 'Edge Hill had done its duty, and had declared itself in favour of Free Trade and the Budget, which opinion was confirmed later by the Nation as a whole'.[37]

Edge Hill may have had a clear idea of what a woman's role was, and was concerned to propagate this image, but the students in their own activities (admittedly held under Edge Hill's aegis) showed a healthy interest in feminism, the suffrage question and other debates of interest to the period. As early as 1894 the College Debating Society decided by 64 to 15 votes 'that the franchise should be extended to women' and against the motion 'that the influence of fashion is demoralising' by a smaller margin of 50 to 43 votes.[38] However, in 1904 the motion that 'Man's intelligence is superior to Woman's' was surprisingly carried by 41 to 36 votes.[39]

Despite Miss Hale's disapproval of feminism in general and the suffragettes in particular,[40] students and former students did display an interest in getting the vote. As well as debating the proposition on a number of occasions, from 1907 there was a steady reference to suffragette activities in the *Edge Hill College Magazine*. In 1907, Ethel Snowden (who, as Ethel Annakin, had been a student from 1900-2) contributed an article on 'Education and the Woman Question'. She herself made reference to the fact that the *Magazine* was actually publishing it:

> the fact that this subject has been selected as entirely proper for such a journal gives the lie once more to those people who are continually taunting us with the charge that the teaching profession is too absorbed in its professional work to take an intelligent interest in anything outside that work.

She pointed out that 'politics generally and the woman question in particular' was vitally connected to teaching. It was important to improve mothers' education and home conditions:

> By means of politics better land laws can be made, better housing, better sanitation, better wages, work for all under decent and honourable conditions, more leisure for self-improvement, temperance legislation and help for the aged—all these can be secured … the voices of the nation's women should be heard; but they are silent. Women have to share in this work, simply because they are women. Never a question comes before Parliament but it has some bearing on the sphere which is to be the woman's, the home; or it affects in some way, the woman herself. Yet she has no say in the ordering of her life and that of her children.

She ended with a stirring cry that teachers should rise up and demand the enfranchisement of women.

On 25 January 1908 the prospective Liverpool City Councillor, Ellen Robinson, addressed the Guild on 'The Present Political and Social Status of Women' and advocated the suffrage for women.[41] In March it was reported that 'College was represented in the audience' at the Picton Lecture Hall to hear Mrs. Fawcett and the former Edge Hillian, Mrs. Philip Snowden (Ethel Annakin, 1900-2) on 'Woman Suffrage'. These speeches 'were listened to with attention by a crowded meeting'.[42]

Great coverage was given to developments in June 1908. Two articles were devoted to them: one by Kathleen Ratcliffe on the Hyde Park Demonstration of 21 June and one by Helena Normanton, who had been one of Edge Hill's most successful university students, having graduated from the University of London with a first-class B.A. Honours degree in History, on the March to Albert Hall on 13 June. She pointed out that 'Edge Hill women must be proud that a distinguished old student, Ethel Snowden (née Annakin), was in the front rank', along with Lady Frances Balfour, Mrs. Fawcett, Miss Emily Davies (who had founded Girton College Cambridge and was now 70 but had presented the first petition to John Stuart Mill in 1865) 'which means to say that for fifty years women have been asking in a nice polite way for this great reform before it dawned on them that they were being made the victims of their own sweet reasonableness! … To all Edge Hill suffragists I give the advice—it takes no moral courage whatever to walk in a procession!'. This was an outright call to militancy and contrasted very much with the views of Miss Hale. Despite Miss Hale's reservations, interest continued. On 23 March 1912 Ethel Snowden gave a 'forcible address on Woman Suffrage' to the Guild and the Home Reading Association meeting 'to an enthusiastic gathering and the discussion which followed proved that keen interest is taken in this subject'.[43]

**29** *The staff, July 1910*

Miss Hale's arguments had always reiterated those of the opponents of women's suffrage and her attitude when women did get the vote was no different:

> It is the duty of every voter to consider carefully what this new privilege means—for there is no privilege without accompanying responsibility. That the influence of women however felt hitherto, is now to be recognised as a factor in the state, is of the utmost importance, but it must be exercised for the good of the community as a whole, not in the interest of any one party or sex …[44]

Articles in the *College Magazine*, however, continued to press women's claims to equality and to take issue with the idea that women would become some sort of man-hating viragos. Thus Theresa A. Smith in an article on 'Woman and Home Life in Norway' pointed out that 'Conditions in Norway defeat the argument that chivalry will disappear when women hold public positions previously allocated to men … the opposite obtains, for then she holds his respect as a comrade and an equal'.[45]

★ ★ ★

Edge Hill, then, stood in a commanding position at the start of the First World War. It had established a strong academic tradition and aimed to provide as stimulating an environment as possible for its students who on the whole appeared to enjoy and flourish under the experience. They had a sense of pride and corporate attachment to Edge Hill.

# 3
# WORLD WAR ONE

**30**  *Students, 1914-16*

War seemed to touch the internal workings of Edge Hill little. In the *Report* of 1914-15 Miss Hale related that 'indirect services, time and money have been fully given to help in the nation's need'. She also maintained that, 'A sympathetic and intelligent interest in current events has been stimulated by literature dealing with the war, its causes and probable effects, and by addresses, notably one given by a Belgian lady, Madame Biemé, on Belgium, and another by an Alsatian, the Counte de Croze, on Alsace'. Not all of this, however, fell on receptive ears: interest in current affairs was not a noted characteristic of the average Edge Hillian:[1]

> I [Edna Walker 1915-17] do not remember either buying or seeing a paper so we were not aware of the stupendous events in Gallipoli, nor the collapse of Russia, nor Zeppelins over London, nor the use of the war-winning weapon, the tank.

Perhaps such 'ignorance' is not surprising if Miss Hale delivered all her addresses in such terms as the following:

> By careful and diligent preparation for their profession, by keeping well and fit for whatever occasion may offer, by cheerfulness and undaunted courage, by the endeavour to realise more and more fully that it is the sense of individual responsibility that makes for character, and not mere

mechanical obedience—that the highest life is sacrifice—it is hoped that Students and Staff may render, in this time of strain and stress, bounden duty and effective service to our beloved Country and the Empire.[2]

Indeed, as Edna Walker (1915-17) said, 'Probably Miss Hale's discourses were excellent but her voice was low and attention was apt to wander …'

The students were aware that their existence might seem very self-contained.

It may seem to those who read the following pages that the Great War has made little or no difference to us, but that is far from being the case. In addition to the numerous 'War Works' which have been carried on by all with unabated energy and enthusiasm, there *is* a difference in the very attitude of mind brought to bear on the ordinary things of life—these are hereby invested with new interest, and the sense of proportion with reference to their value is materially changed. There are such big things at stake that material interests count for little in comparison. As far as can be perceived, life *is* going on 'as usual', includes much that has not always been included and much that is of inestimable value in promoting the welfare of England's future citizens, with whom our work is mainly concerned.[3]

To help the war effort Miss Hale urged all to buy War Savings Certificates and to encourage thrift. Twice Edge Hill entertained soldiers from a local hospital to a 'gorgeous feast'. Relations were somewhat strained because 'the soldiers were shy; until a regrettably vulgar comic from their midst lowered the tone, but raised the spirits of the entire gathering. I can still see Miss Howe's face with that "we are not amused" expression. After that, however, things went with a bang and the soldiers danced and sang with the students and really enjoyed themselves'. A second occasion proved a 'flop'. Food was provided for 70 but only seven turned up, a local cup tie proving more attractive. 'But for the hungry students it was a Field Day' (Edna Walker, 1915-17).

Women were now needed ever-increasingly to teach boys and students did teaching practice in boys schools. Miss Hale, however, was not convinced of the equality of women '… one does not contemplate with satisfaction the dearth of men teachers. However well the women teachers succeed in the management of boys, they need more of virile quality to make them really efficient, especially for the older scholars'.[4]

Former students played a very varied role in the war effort. A sample of 170 Guild members (admittedly very small) revealed that 80 were engaged in National Registration and Recruiting. All were subscribing in one way or another to a variety of war funds: among which were the Prince of Wales Fund, Red Cross Society, Belgian and Serbian Relief, Prisoners of War Fund and Star and Garter Fund for Disabled Soldiers. They helped to raise money through flag days, house to house collections, provided clothing for the troops (one had knitted over 300 pairs of socks), made crutches, lockers and bed tables for hospitals. Some had taken up nursing, others distributed relief to the forces' families.

The war brought financial hardship; by 1918 Edge Hill was 'greatly relieved' that the Treasury grant was to be increased, 'for, in spite of raising the entrance fee and of ultra economical management on the part of our invaluable Mrs. Evans, we were likely to find ourselves in a tight place had not this addition come most opportunely'.[5]

Physical conditions were deteriorating: the autumn of 1918 saw a water shortage, leaking pipes, the heating breaking down and a flu epidemic in September with another in February 1919. It was becoming more and more obvious that the institution needed to be expanded and it was planned to extend the Clint Road wing to give more classroom and dormitory accommodation and more suitable quarters for staff. Miss Hale appealed to old students to contribute.

Armistice (11 November 1918) was greeted with great relief by the students. It was a 'never-to-be-forgotten' day in the annals of College since it ended the 'terrible slaughter that for more than four years had been devastating the world'. The afternoon was made a holiday and the evening a college sing-song 'composed chiefly of national and patriotic songs which gave an outlet for the relief and excitement which were so strongly felt by all'.[6]

Academically there had been one major alteration during the war years. The character of the examination was changed in 1915 when there were to be two grades of papers—'Ordinary' and 'Advanced'—in the Required Subjects. Subjects previously known as 'Optional' were to be called 'Additional'. A 'pass with credit' was available in the Required Subjects and a 'pass with distinction' in Advanced and Additional papers. This gave an incentive to the good student to work hard, and could be said to be the Board's first attempt at distinguishing between those intending to teach primary and those older children.

Edge Hill approved: it would give wider choice of the non-Professional subjects (i.e. those other than English, mathematics, history, geography and elementary science). 'The new conditions have apparently worked well; the better students have been able to use their time more freely and with advantages whilst the less able have concentrated on fewer subjects and have not been unduly pressed'.[7]

The Fisher Education Act of 1918, which now *inter alia* raised the school leaving age to 14 and made larger grants to local authorities to enable them to increase teachers' salaries, was greeted by Miss Hale with enthusiasm: 'There are many signs that the nation is awakening to the value and importance of Education, and to the fact that not only is the labourer worthy of his hire, but is himself worthy … when it becomes effective it should do much towards establishing Education on sounder and more complete lines than heretofore'. Better salaries should attract many, therefore remedying the present shortage of teachers. At the same time a note of realism was sounded: 'The shortage of teachers, the insufficiency of Educational machinery, the ineptitude and inertia of many Local Education Authorities will sadly hamper the Bill'.

Despite this, Miss Hale had no doubts that conditions in training colleges had improved over the last 40 years: 'it is indubitable that the training now given to the intending teacher is altogether on more reasonable lines'.[8] As always Edge Hill appeared to be in advance of official thinking, since several of the proposed changes had already been adopted; e.g. the University of Liverpool examined students for their Certificate instead of the Board of Education. This had worked quite satisfactorily for nine years except for the financial side, since Edge Hill was responsible for all the expenses. From 1919 the University's Senate Training College Committee and the Board of Education were to approve syllabuses, examination papers and final results in a system which covered Edge Hill, Warrington and Chester Colleges. This was to cost each institution £100 a year.

Miss Hale had successfully guided Edge Hill through the war years. Her thinking, however, was firmly rooted in the Victorian era, laying great stress on duty and service. She was outraged at industrial action. Having stated at the beginning of *Notes from the Principal 1919* that 'I must not emulate the daily papers in animadverting upon the present discontent from which alas! even our own profession is not exempt', three pages later in the same article she delivered a blistering attack on teachers' strikes which is worth quoting in its entirety:

The discontent at insufficient pay leading in some quarters to strikes, is a grave reflection on the profession. I greatly deprecate such extreme measures, which cannot but have a bad effect on both children and parents, and would seem to imply that the welfare of the children is not the chief interest of the teacher. The country is indeed very far from realising the Christian ideal of altruism, and certain sections appear to be bent on obtaining by force whatever it [sic] desires without considering the general effect upon the population. A strike is after all a *boomerang*, and will sooner or later return to vex the strikers. How can teachers meet this evil of a selfish industrialism? Certainly not by adopting similar methods,—but by endeavouring to train their pupils into a nobler ideal of citizenship—to look not on their own things only but also on the things that make for the good of others—to consider that whilst the good of the community re-acts beneficially on the individual, the selfish interests of the individual may be inimical to the good of the community. The basic idea of all revolutions is that many suffer for the advantage of the few; to counteract this it is necessary to get all classes of the community to realise that they must work together for the good of all. The pre-war class distinctions are giving place to what is perhaps, a more serious evil—strife between employer and employed; the latter envying the profits on the use of capital, not considering in their ignorance of economics that these go to make more capital for the use of labour; the former through greed and selfishness denying to the employed sufficient return for their labour. Hence Capital and Labour, which are useless the one without the other, are continually in a conflict which tends to their mutual undoing. Ignorance is not confined to the one side: the study of economics and civics have [sic] been too grossly neglected, hence confusion dissatisfaction and strife. Teachers must see to it that the rising generation is more fully instructed in these matters—they are the things that concern life.

Miss Hale therefore very evidently belonged to the 19th century. She had no real idea of the basis of class or the fact that class had been a factor in politics for some considerable time. From her comfortable salary of £485 p.a. it was easy to say that strikes were selfish and to counsel altruism in a rather condescending fashion. Her life-style was cushioned: 'Here in my pleasant summer retreat on a Yorkshire moor there is but a faint echo of the world turbulence'; even in war time her personal maid waited behind her chair during meals.

By the end of Miss Hale's principalship Edge Hill had come a long way. It was firmly established as an institution of the first rank. It had trained 2,071 girls of whom in 1920 213 were Head Mistresses, 178 First Assistants and 30 science mistresses (see Table X).

A tribute to Miss Hale classed her as 'ever progressive, and never afraid of innovation, whilst at the same time severely critical'. She was certainly outspoken but it is difficult to describe her as 'ever progressive'; she reacted to trends rather than innovated. Her response to outside events tended to be that of a patriotic conservative—indeed she had been a bulwark of the Conservative Club while a student at Newnham College Cambridge—and this was the type of philosophy that she promoted in her students.[9] When Ladysmith was relieved during the Boer War, the girls were given a half holiday and were encouraged to celebrate subsequent successes:

> We 'mafficked' on the night of May 18th, though we had to content ourselves with sitting up the spiral staircase to listen to the horns and whistles, and with ringing all the college bells at once, till we were brought in and allowed to let off more steam in decorating the dining room with red, white and blue draperies, patriotic devices, and portraits of illustrious generals.[10]

The emphasis was on service and duty: service to the wider community with a duty to help those in need.

## TABLE X
### Position at 1920

| | * | Head Mistress | First Mistress | Assistant | Science Mistress | HMI |
|---|---|---|---|---|---|---|
| 1885-6 | (41) | 10 | | 1 | | |
| 1886-7 | (40) | 8 | 1 | 4 | 1 | |
| 1887-8 | (41) | 10 | 1 | | 1 | |
| 1888-9 | (39) | 8 | | | | |
| 1889-90 | (40) | 11 | | | | |
| 1890-1 | (39) | 11 | 6 | 2 | | |
| 1891-2 | (41) | 8 | 5 | 3 | 1 | |
| 1892-3 | (47) | 9 | 8 | 3 | | |
| 1893-4 | (55) | 11 | 6 | 5 | | |
| 1894-5 | (53) | 16 | 3 | 6 | 1 | |
| 1895-6 | (56) | 13 | 4 | 18 | | |
| 1895-6-7 | (53) | 12 | 5 | 8 | | |
| 1896-7-8 | (53) | 8 | 4 | 7 | 1 | |
| 1897-8-9 | (57) | 16 | 4 | 12 | | |
| 1898-1900 | (55) | 9 | 3 | 11 | | 1 |
| 1899-1901 | (52) | 8 | 4 | 9 | 2 | |
| 1900-2 | (63) | 9 | 6 | 10 | 1 | 1 |
| 1901-3 | (53) | 6 | 12 | 19 | | |
| 1902-4 | (61) | 7 | 8 | 18 | | |
| 1903-5 | (57) | 3 | 6 | 21 | 1 | |
| 1904-6 | (68) | 5 | 5 | 31 | 1 | |
| 1905-7 | (66) | 1 | 2 | 20 | 1 | |
| 1906-8 | (69) | 3 | 4 | 32 | 1 | |
| 1907-9 | (75) | 4 | 7 | 36 | 3 | |
| 1908-10 | (72) | 2 | 7 | 33 | 4 | |
| 1909-11 | (75) | 4 | 1 | 42 | 2 | |
| 1910-12 | (68) | | 1 | 44 | 3 | |
| 1911-13 | (75) | 1 | 2 | 51 | 3 | |
| 1912-14 | (64) | | | 48 | | |
| 1913-15 | (76) | | 2 | 65 | 5 | |
| 1914-16 | (69) | | | 65 | | |
| 1915-17 | (78) | | | 78 | | |
| 1916-18 | (70) | | 1 | 62 | 3 | |
| 1917-19 | (77) | | 1 | 73 | | |
| 1918-20 | (71) | | | 59 | | |

* Numbers in brackets refer to those who actually sought work

**31**  *The Children's Party, 1912*

Feminism was not encouraged; indeed a belief in full-time careers for women is definitely lacking. Despite the many deficiencies of the *Registers* as a source of evidence, there is one piece of information which is always recorded in great detail: the date of a former student's marriage and the number of children she produced. Each *Directory* also makes great play of the numbers who got married. Matrimony therefore would still seem to be the career as far as the staff was concerned; teaching was second best. Edge Hill thus reinforced contemporary mores; a woman's *real* place was in the home. This message was also strengthened by glowing reports of gatherings of mothers and children. 'There could not be a brighter, happier, healthier looking set of youngsters anywhere and they bear testimony to the fact that Edge Hill has trained good mothers, no less than good teachers.'[11] Teaching therefore was a convenient profession for tiding a woman over till she married, though Miss Hale did support equal pay for women teachers:

> It is terrible heresy, no doubt, and would lead to a great upheaval in the present order of things, but why also should not a *woman* teacher be paid at the same rate as a *man*? She does the same kind of work, puts in more rather than less, hours per day, and may be as highly certificated. Even when she is working under precisely the same conditions, say as Assistant in a boys' department, her salary falls very much below that of her fellow-assistant, just because he is a man, and for no other reason.[12]

Indeed this was the one area in which she appeared quite radical. She returned to the question of salaries regularly; thus in 1913 she maintained:

> The average salary of the assistant and of too many head teachers ranks below that of the ordinary clerk, yet the preparation is more costly in time and energy and the nervous strain of the work is incomparably greater. I think that Local Education Authorities are not studying the highest interest of education in seeking to reduce expenditure, by keeping down salaries, by using unqualified teachers and and by employing a minimum staff.

And in 1919 she rejoiced in the provision of a 'liberal' pension scheme.

Such attitudes help to explain her disapproval of the suffragettes:

> Women will come into their rights, nay, they may now enjoy even political rights in effect if not in law, by exercising a wisely quiet and tenderly wise influence over those with whom they are in

communication—not by wildly shrieking forth their woes, real or fancied. I am very grateful to Dr. Watson who, in his charge to the students who left this year, urged them to bear in mind that they as women teachers, and teachers of those who would presently be the women of England had it greatly in their power to mould the character of its people and therefore to influence the country for good or evil. In this way all women can, in the words of Mazzini, 'Hasten the redemption of woman, by restoring her to her mission of Inspiration, Prayer and Piety, so divinely symbolised by Christianity in Mary'.

Her achievement was that she had kept Edge Hill on an even keel. There is no doubt that Miss Hale had great presence; most of the students stood in awe of her. A.M. Edna Walker (1915-17) remembered in 1978:

> Miss Hale was a very great lady; to most of us a remote and powerful presence, yet to anyone in real distress she could be infinitely kind. Her mental capacity and her ability to deal with the many difficulties that war time brought were without parallel. She was really an old lady, 66 years old when I left College, but neither her demeanour nor her dress showed it. There was never any doubt that she was 'The Principal'.

She was nevertheless seeking retirement at the right time; it is doubtful whether she could have coped with the problems of the post-war world. It was unfortunate, however, that she died on 1 April 1920 *before* her well-earned retirement began. Many tributes of appreciation paid testimony to the respect and loyalty that she inspired and a large number felt that their 'loved and esteemed Head would have preferred her call to the Higher Life to come as it did, while she was still in harness'.

She was succeeded by Miss E.M. Smith who had an impeccable academic record. Educated at Newnham College Cambridge, where she took a First in mathematics and achieved a position equal to the 16th wrangler, she then had a year in America as fellow in mathematics at Bryn Mawr College. On returning to England she was appointed maths mistress at Cheltenham Ladies College, a position she held from 1910 to 1916 and was then Head Mistress of Rotherham Municipal High School from 1916 to 1920.

# 4
# BETWEEN THE WARS

In the immediate post-war years all training colleges were prevented from expansion by lack of finance. Edge Hill increased its fees to £25 and received a larger grant from the Board of Education. But still a 'very large burden of debt … hangs heavily around our necks, and it is not yet clear how it can be removed'.[1] New premises therefore were out of the question, though the building fund was active.

The general slump in the economy led to cuts in government expenditure among which was a reduction of staffing in schools. This of course made it harder for students to find employment. Miss Smith noted with 'grave concern' in 1923 that large numbers of girls who had been urged to take up teaching had not succeeded in gaining a place in training colleges and therefore had to take posts as 'uncertificated' teachers 'and in these days of economy there are not enough posts to go round'.[2] In the nationwide cut in student numbers Edge Hill's fell from 160 to 153.

The buildings and amenities of the institution, however, were causing growing concern. The Minute Books record constant problems with the boilers and other items of costly maintenance. It was gradually realised that what was wanted was an entirely new college; the cost, however, would be enormous. The Committee therefore began to sound out the Board of Education as to whether it would supply the money in one form or another. The reply was unequivocal: 'Financial assistance could not be given unless grants were made by local authorities, and then only under certain circumstance'. Accordingly the Committee decided that 'nothing further be done for the present'.[3]

Nevertheless, events were now taken out of Edge Hill's hands: the 1925 Board of Education report completely condemned the building and site 'as it is now'. Conditions for staff and students had to be improved, and this would only be achieved with a new building in a new location. Such an enterprise required State assistance which would only come through a local authority. The Committee therefore agreed to hand over Edge Hill to Lancashire Education Committee 'on the distinct understanding that a new building is to be provided as soon as possible' and that continuity in terms of name, history and reputation was to be preserved. The new governing body included a large portion of the old Committee and kept as its Chairman, Mrs. Charles Booth.

This was no mean bargain for Lancashire: it was acquiring a well established college with around 160 places at a time when it was highly unlikely that the Board of Education would agree to an entirely new creation. Edge Hill was not, however, to become flooded with county students; while the institution remained at the old premises admissions were not to be confined solely to these students. In practice they normally accounted for less than 42 per cent (e.g. 1927, 39%; 1940, 17%).

Lancashire did its best to welcome Edge Hill. The Chairman of the Education Committee, J.T. Travis-Clegg, sent a warm letter to Guild members through the *College Magazine*. He was

32    *The dining hall*

33    *Housecraft room*

*34    Edge Hill College, Ormskirk*

'aware that Edge Hill Training College has honourable traditions and a great reputation built up during the past 40 years' and hoped that under 'new conditions, with modern buildings and proper Playing Field accommodation … all the traditions of the past will be maintained, the reputation of the College will be enhanced and its usefulness increased'.[4] Lancashire became tenants of the Durning Road site at a nominal rent.

The existing building, however, still caused costly problems: in 1928 the institution had to be re-wired at much expense 'owing to the dangerous state of the electrical system'.[5] It still lacked adequate heating; indeed students used a rudimentary heating duct for getting rid of the dust from their cubicles: 'We … swept the bits down a grating which ran down the centre of the corridor. This was supposed to be for a kind of central heating but as no heat ever came up we used it for dust. So with no other heat it was terribly cold in the winter' (N. Aldred, 1925-7). It must have been a great relief when Lancashire Education Committee bought 34 acres of the present site at Ormskirk. Miss Smith reported delightedly: 'When I first saw it, hares were disporting themselves upon it, and I like to think of the rural aspect which this gives to what will be our surroundings'. Unspoken fears of the isolated nature of the place were dispelled when it was found that it was only 15 minutes from the station 'and omnibuses run in all directions … Southport, Wigan, St Helens and Liverpool are within short distances, so that we shall not be cut off too much from the amenities of the city and from variety of schools'.[6]

The foundation stone was laid on 26 October 1931 by J.T. Travis-Clegg, Chairman of Lancashire County Council. The new buildings (which were a prime example of 1930s architecture), consisted of a main education block, four halls of residence to accommodate 50 students and four staff and a dining hall for two hundred and fifty. The education block housed an Assembly Hall, library, craft rooms, gymnasium, music rooms, lecture and classrooms. There was also an indoor swimming pool presented by the Trustees of the Old College and the Guild gave £1,500 to decorate the College Hall to be known as the Hale Memorial Hall (Hale Hall). The halls of residence were to be named Stanley, Clough, Lady Margaret and John Dalton 'in honour' of the Derby family and 'of three individuals famous in the history of Lancashire and of Education' (Ann Jemima Clough was a pioneer of higher education for women, having founded Newnham College Cambridge).

The building was opened on 2 October 1933 by Lord Irwin, President of the Board of Education. Speakers laid emphasis on educating the *whole* individual: 'we want in our teachers vivid personalities in healthy bodies, able to enjoy all kinds of physical activity, and we want also sensitiveness to beauty and to the dignity of simple, orderly living'. It was 'more important to teach people how to think than what to think'. And, perhaps reflecting the depression's effects on employment opportunities, 'children and adolescents must be trained to enjoy their leisure time also with pleasure and profit'.[7] There was a service of commemoration at Liverpool Cathedral where the preacher was Professor Rains of Cambridge. Edge Hill now consisted of 180 students with four resident maids for each hall.

One of the greatest boons from the students' point of view was the extensive grounds. They played a full role in developing these, helping particularly in laying them out.[8] As well as lawns, playing fields and beautiful floral displays, they offered a kitchen garden which in its first year provided gooseberries, radishes, spinach and potatoes—the latter exceeded Edge Hill's requirements by 20 tons and were to be sold![9]

The Durning Road premises were eventually purchased by Liverpool Education Department for £6,000, the net proceeds to be used to pay for the swimming pool. A German bombing raid on 28 November 1940 scored a direct hit on the original Edge Hill where around 200 people sheltering in the cellars died either of scalding or drowning when the boilers burst.

★ ★ ★

Financial difficulties were not the only problems besetting training colleges in the immediate post-war years. Not all were convinced of their value as teacher educators. One major criticism was that the colleges laid too much stress on theory to the neglect of the practical skill of teaching. The *Times Educational Supplement* took this view in a series of articles published in July 1918. There was a widespread assumption that in the limited period of two years far too much was attempted with the result that the student never really tackled any subject on anything other than a superficial level. It could certainly be argued that the curriculum was overloaded and that the students found themselves with very little time for private study. It was almost a case of the 'Devil makes mischief for idle hands'. Edge Hill had always taken great pride in its reputation for hard work; at its 25th anniversary it was stated with admiration, 'Edge Hill has never been a comfortable, easy depot for folk who think it would be nice to get a little education. On the contrary, it has always been characterised by stern endeavour, hard work, and unwearied perseverance'.[10]

Oral evidence in 1984 from Eve Johnson (1927-9) relates 'relaxation and leisure were unknown words'. The staff, however, did take the problem of leisure seriously. Eve Johnson again:

We did have a lot of work to get through, and leisure was forced upon us in that we were forced to go out walking, during the afternoon, to get fresh air. We were in trouble if caught working in the Science room or Library when we should have been walking the pavements of Edge Hill worrying about the amount of work to be done later …

Life under Miss Smith did illustrate the strange mixture of strictness and laxity which characterised much of training college existence. Well-qualified herself, she had very much her own ideas about the qualifications needed by intending students. At interview, she told Dorothy Fox (née Elliot) to drop her 'A' level subjects and concentrate on needlework and art. 'To my dismay the comment of the Headmaster was that while Miss Smith ran Edge Hill he ran Fleetwood Grammar and that I should continue with my studies. How glad I have been since then that he so advised.'

Mrs. Fox paints a very good picture of Miss Smith. She 'was a terrifying figure. With hindsight one respects her but then one feared her. She always wore long black dresses and walked with a stick. Her black hair was in a bun and because of her bad eyesight she had thick pebble lenses'. Having to sit on the Principal's table was a 'nightmare'. Latecomers had to sit next to her and the 'thought of having to make conversation with her was daunting'.

Despite this the staff were not above making fun of her: 'Miss Barr (PE) was giving us a lecture on posture. She jumped onto the table and imitated various postures ending by imitating Miss Smith's walk. We roared with laughter and the door opened and in came Pip Emma [Miss Smith] to complain about the noise. We wondered how Miss Barr felt up on the table'.

And discipline in lectures was certainly very lax: 'It was common practice to knit during lectures in the large lecture theatre and occasionally there would be the metallic clang of a falling knitting needle. There would be a bustle while knitting was hastily hidden as the lecturer came up the aisle to investigate' (D. Fox, 1938-40).

Nevertheless, despite her awesome reputation, Miss Smith seems to have given requests for more freedom serious consideration. Given the apprehension on the part of the staff about men coming into contact with the students, it is perhaps surprising to learn that 1924-5 saw the institution of the 'male dance'. Kathleen Beswick (née Bell, 1923-5) 'plucked up enough courage to ask Miss E.M. Smith, Principal, if we could invite men to our Christmas Dance and if we could wear coloured evening dresses. Hitherto, our evening dresses were all white, and we had had no men for partners. We just danced with each other'. Permission was given and men imported from Chester Training College, two of whom later married Edge Hill students. Guests had to receive a formal invitation and on arrival were marched up and introduced to Miss Smith. 'The Staff were briefed to ensure that couples did not stray beyond the Hall, but I [Catherine Campbell, 1932-4] remember that I managed to get as far as the bicycle shed with my partner only to be discovered by Miss Butterworth with her torch!' It was small wonder that some ex-students described it as 'a convent'.

Former students, reminiscing, were certainly aware of the lack of responsibility. Nevertheless, Edge Hill was no cultural desert; a wide variety of clubs and societies existed, external lecturers came regularly, and the library was steadily expanded. Furthermore, attempts were made to reduce stress on students. From 1921 University students were to spend a fourth year at Edge Hill; this was to be used for their professional training and it was hoped that it would reduce the strains of preparing for both Finals and teaching qualifications. Edge Hill was now in line with the universities.

*Ormskirk, The Assembly Hall, Edge Hill College.*
*FRITH. OMK.19*

**35** *The assembly hall*

**36** *A student's room*

*Ormskirk, A Student's Room, Edge Hill College.*
*FRITH. OMK.22*

The late 1920s saw changes in the conduct of the Certificate examinations. From 1929 an examination board representing the universities and the training colleges was to be responsible for the final examinations. Membership of this board consisted of representatives of the eight training colleges and of the Universities of Liverpool and Manchester. External examiners were appointed and the first examinations under the new system were to take place in 1930. The Board of Education paid £1.50 per candidate and the student £2.50. Miss Smith commented, 'This type of examination is very expensive, and it is not certain yet that the fee of £4 per head will cover the cost'.[11] Edge Hill therefore proceeded cautiously; the only change it proposed was to allow students to offer two subsidiary or professional courses instead of one ordinary course. All students already took such courses in their first year but previously these had not been formally examined. The proposed subjects were to be mathematics, geography, history and science.

The results of the first examination proved 'quite satisfactory' with two fails, 21 distinctions, 53 credits and 54 passes. Miss Smith now looked on the new system rather more favourably: 'We see a tendency to increase the number of tests, and we may expect to see a raising of the standard of requirement for passing. It is of course in the interest of the nation that the qualifications of its teachers should be as high as possible'.[12]

The Depression's effects on education continued throughout the 1930s. In response to a fall in the school population and the increasing tendency to employ cheaper, less qualified teachers, the Board of Education continually reduced college admissions from 1932-5. In 1932-3 places were cut by two per cent, in 1933-4 by a further 10 per cent and in 1934-5 by eight per cent. Nationally this meant one woman in three did not secure a place. Edge Hill found its numbers reduced from 160 to 156 in 1932-3; 75 were admitted in 1932. The further reductions meant that admissions for 1933-4 would be 68; thus a building intended for 200 would house only one hundred and forty-three. Special permission therefore was granted to admit ninety. A similar plea was made in the following year and in fact 166 places were filled over the next three years.

Unemployment, however, remained a problem; of the 1935 leavers, 14 out of 98 were without jobs by December 1935, eight out of 69 in 1936, 10 out of 96 in 1937, seven out of 67 in 1938. A large number only secured temporary appointments: 32 in 1935, 17 in 1936, 23 in 1937, six in 1938.

**TABLE XI**

| Date | Total Students | Permanent | Temporary | Unemployed | Further Course |
|---|---|---|---|---|---|
| 1935 | 98 | 52 | 32 | 14 | |
| 1936 | 69 | 42 | 17 | 8 | 2 |
| 1937 | 96 | 60 | 23 | 10 | 3 |
| 1938 | 67 | 54 | 6 | 7 | |

Lack of employment prospects obviously affected recruitment: in 1937 Edge Hill had 41 vacant places. A bumper admission of 103 in 1938, however, left only eight vacancies. Edge Hill nevertheless continued to develop its courses: in 1937 advanced physical education was begun. This 'aroused much interest'. A third-year course in art was to be recognised from September 1937 but the outbreak of war stopped further change.

# 5
# THE YEARS AT BINGLEY

It was as late as May 1939 before the Principal was informed that, in the event of war, Edge Hill's buildings would be requisitioned. As soon as mobilisation took place (3 September) soldiers moved in. Under the war-time arrangements, Edge Hill was to share a college at Bingley in Yorkshire. Accordingly they left on 4 September after a very hasty removal (some property went to Bingley, the rest went into store in Widnes).

The Edge Hill timetable was tailored to fit Bingley commitments so that both colleges could use the classrooms, the gym and the field. This enabled usual programmes to be followed and college societies to function. Edge Hill was to occupy two of the five halls of residence. Ill health and increasing sight difficulties forced Miss Smith to retire at the end of the summer term 1941. Miss Butterworth was appointed acting Principal at a salary of £400 for the duration of the war. A temporary appointment seemed most apt because a suitable candidate might not want to leave her present work, and conditions at Bingley would have been difficult for a new Principal.

The 1942 session brought a number of changes: there was to be no Staff Hall (since Bingley wished to increase its student numbers from 162 to 180, all accommodation was needed); all five halls were to be used by both staff and students, a few staff becoming non-resident. The Chairman of the West Riding Education Department suggested that staff accommodation might be forthcoming in the town because 'it is thought that residents in the town of Bingley would welcome the opportunity of providing living quarters for such persons as an alternative to having billeted on them evacuees who require full board and might in other aspects too be less desirable guests'.[1]

Priestly Hall housed what would have been Stanley and Clough, and Acland, John Dalton and Lady Margaret; some students were scattered among all five halls. Conditions were very cramped: two students in a room designed for one containing two beds, one desk, one wardrobe and one octagonal two-tiered table where the drawers were shared. There was therefore a great lack of privacy and, if one was forced to share with someone uncongenial, much unhappiness could result.[2] The day was to be rescheduled 'to meet the needs of the domestic arrangement'. There were to be classes in the morning (9.30 to 12 noon) and afternoon (1.00 to 4.00; 5.00 to 6.00) instead of the evening. This would ensure an uninterrupted period which could be used for private study and the College societies. Lectures were also held on Saturday mornings.[3]

The rising bell rang at 7.00 a.m. and immediately there was a queue for the washing facilities. The solution was: either get up *before* 7.00 a.m. or miss breakfast and wash then. Restrictions and regulations were many. Students were not expected to go out during the week. At the weekends they had to be in by 8.00 p.m. (extended in the 1944-5 session to 9.00 p.m.). If a student was going out, she had to state her destination in the Hall Warden's book and the time she was expected back. On dark nights they had to return in threes. The regulations had not really changed in character from those of the 1890s. Students' reactions, however, had to some extent: they flouted the lights-out restrictions by covering the skylight with a thick grey blanket. Many of the students also felt ill at ease: 'As "guests" of another college, Edge Hill had to make do with second best in many ways and be particularly careful not to upset our "hosts". A tricky situation even more for the staff than the students …'.[4]

War-time brought its own problems: there were not enough schools for teaching practice and transport was limited; there was a lack of suitable applicants for the teaching profession; numbers had been limited to 160 for the period at Bingley, but by 1942 Edge Hill had only one hundred and thirty-eight. By 1943 students could enter college at 17+ instead of 18+. Almost half of those admitted in 1944 were under eighteen. Basically this meant that they did not have to have the Higher School Certificate. 'Their background of knowledge would be less and it might be wise to attempt fewer Advanced Courses than in the past.'[5] Miss Butterworth in the *Newsletter* repeatedly lamented the lack of the 'right sort of candidate'. Not all were committed to teaching. At 18 a girl was liable for national service and some chose to take up teaching (a reserved occupation) to avoid this. The shortage of domestic staff meant that students had to do an ever increasing amount of domestic/household tasks for themselves. Miss Butterworth optimistically told the Governors in 1942 that the students were enjoying their 'Housewife' turns. 'They had accepted the situation happily and the arrangements had been a great success.' Mary Bancroft (1943-5) looking back in 1969, however, probably sums up the students' reactions more accurately:

> Apart from cleaning our own rooms (banging threadbare mats on the steps on Saturday mornings) twice a term one would have a day on 'housework' with one's room-mate. We were excused lectures while we swept and dusted, cleared the tables and set them again, doled out tea and buns in the afternoon and milk in the evening. Housework was not very popular but even less so was work in the main kitchens which was necessary once for a few weeks when there was a strike of kitchen staff. Oh, those horrible pans to scrape and piles of lettuce to wash and search for caterpillars, but the kitchen work was only temporary, thank goodness.[6]

There was certainly hostility to the idea; at one point the students 'proclaimed a strike against sharing household chores, and had to be reminded that the only alternative was a visit to the Labour Exchange to be drafted into factories'.[7]

Nevertheless, courses and examinations proceeded much as usual and a wide range of extra-curricular activities including games, outside lectures, dramatic performances and the normal student societies was maintained. Miss Buxbaum was seconded to the ATS as a PT Officer. Students were also trained in First Aid and the staff and second years took courses to qualify as Air Raid Wardens. The vacations were spent doing national service: everything from fruit picking to munitions, hospital work to war nurseries.[8] Red Cross activities continued throughout: in 1945 they gave £146 for POW parcels and the two colleges raised a total of £602 between 1941 and 1945.[9]

In preparation for the move back to Ormskirk in Spring 1946 an extra 51 students were admitted. They spent the autumn teaching in their local areas and became resident at Ormskirk in January 1946. Numbers were further increased to 280 for the 1946 session. Lancashire Education Authority was adapting the temporary buildings constructed during the war to make students' rooms, classrooms and a hall for resident domestic help 'whom we still hope to find'. New courses were to be provided: a Housecraft Course limited to 32 students was designed to produce teachers to cope with problems caused by raising the school-leaving age. The students would take Housecraft as their Advanced Subject and spend a third year in a Domestic Science College; General Science and Social Studies were also being added and a lecturer from Liverpool University's Social Science Department was to help in the setting up of the latter.[10]

Much work was needed to restore Edge Hill to civilian use (the building was de-requisitioned on 5 October 1945). The floors were 'so black that a London firm had to be called in to restore their natural oak colouring'. The kitchens lacked 'machinery', the furniture needed reconditioning and the building redecorating. Nevertheless Miss Butterworth was able to state in 1946 that the buildings were 'almost as beautiful as they were before the war'. The actual removal on 24 January was not without its problems.

> Trunks, which had been delivered, and packages from Widnes and Bingley filled the library and X classroom—there was furniture stacked in the Hall—corridor floors were up, and workmen were everywhere. All drawers and cupboards had to be washed before they could be used; blankets, pillows, mattresses, even bedsteads, had to be distributed, so had carpet and curtains and chairs, and the men had still much of the heavier furniture to place.[11]

Within three days, however, student rooms were allocated and both wings were in use in time for the arrival of the first years on 28 January. Despite major inconvenience—'only half the dining-room could be used, and crockery and cutlery were in short supply'—lectures began on 30 January and group lessons in the schools on 31 January. February 15th saw full assembly for prayers. The realities of the post-war world were in evidence though not yet fully appreciated: all students had to take turns at domestic work and many staff also helped in the kitchens. The resident maids had gone forever. Throughout this period a willingness to 'muck in' and make the best of things was apparent and the speed with which Edge Hill returned to normal was remarkable. The following year Miss Butterworth noted with approval:

> Anyone approaching College from either entrance will now see, instead of the brick extensions that were inharmonious with the main building, charming dark-roofed, cream coloured buildings showing most attractively against the greenery of trees, grass and shrubs. Inside them good-sized study bedrooms have been fitted up and the furniture successfully treated to bring harmony and brightness into the original motley of 'supply'.

The 'Huts' were also occupied (as indeed they still were in the early 1990s!). The increase in numbers to 280, however, meant that conditions were very cramped: first years had to live two to a room for almost the whole session; the new rooms for Housecraft were not ready so 'they practised at first on the staff sitting-rooms, and began upholstering some of the chairs damaged during the war'. The greatest problem was finding enough schools for teaching practice.[12]

Miss Butterworth had proved an auspicious choice for Principal; she was universally liked and her personality did much to ensure a relatively smooth running of the institution while in the difficult conditions of evacuation. Finding a successor to her posed problems. The first advertisement threw up no suitable candidates; the re-advertisement, however, provided Edge Hill with its best qualified Principal yet. Margaret Bain had a first-class Honours degree from Aberdeen University, a doctorate from Paris and 14 years' university teaching (three at Cardiff and 11 at Edinburgh) as well as school experience. It was fortunate that such an able woman had been secured since her principalship was to see Edge Hill develop from a small women's establishment to a large mixed institution.

# 6
# McNAIR AND AFTER

In planning for peace, parliament passed the 1944 Education Act which raised the school leaving age to 15 and made secondary education compulsory. As with the 1870 Education Act this would entail an increase in the number of teachers required. With this in mind the Board of Education had set up the McNair Committee in 1942 to examine teacher training. Its report (1944) was critical: 'what is wrong with the majority of training colleges is their poverty, and all that flows from it'. To some extent this was due to their smallness: in 1938 more than sixty colleges had less than 150 students and only five had more than two hundred. Edge Hill therefore was above average in terms of size but not among the largest. To secure adequate numbers of teachers, three improvements were necessary: 'The field of recruitment must be widened, conditions of service which deter people from becoming teachers must be abolished; and the standing of education must be improved so that a sufficient number of men and women of quality will be attracted to teaching as a profession'. Specific recommendations were made: there should be closer association between the training colleges and the universities (to make the courses more alike); better salaries, improved conditions of service (to raise status); specialist courses in music, arts and PE; and the introduction of a three-year course. The latter was designed to 'foster an academic and social life in the colleges more akin to that of the universities'.

It was, however, easier to plan than to change in practice and the shortage of teachers after 1945 meant the postponement of the Three Year Certificate Course. By 1956 a firm decision had been taken to introduce this in 1960. Edge Hill was pleased: student opinion in 1957 had reacted favourably—'A good thing, this three year course in 1960. We have no sooner got into College, settled down to work and had our first school practice than here we are in our second year, with finals and application for posts just around the corner! We need a year between, just to get on with our training!'[1]

Unfortunately the Principal's Reports for the 1940s, '50s and early '60s are not available. Evidence from governors' meetings, however, suggests that Edge Hill had no idea of what the introduction of a three-year course would mean in reality. In early 1957 they were negotiating with the Ministry to secure additional teaching and improved residential accommodation and ensure that 'proposals should be put forward embodying any modifications required for a three year course'.[2] On 29 October 1957 they decided to 'press' the Ministry to agree to an institution of 'approximately 260 students on educational grounds' even if this would require modification of the original building plan; that is, they aimed for a *reduction* in numbers.

The Ministry's decision to *increase* the intake in 1959 therefore must have come as a great shock especially as this was to be achieved by the admission of day students and the use of hostels as temporary buildings. Expansion was needed because of the amount of wastage among women teachers; earlier marriages meant a significant proportion were lost each year. In response the Governors agreed: firstly to step up admissions in 1958 by an additional 15 resident students and 'up to a further 15 if applications were received from suitable local girls who could live at home'; secondly they recommended that Edge Hill should become a *mixed* college of *c.*400 (the first men were to arrive in October 1959) and that the accommodation needed for this should be provided as soon as possible, temporary accommodation being limited where possible to teaching; and thirdly they asked the Ministry for the necessary extra staff. By October the College was to have 480 students and enquiries were being made about acquiring extra land.

The additional year and the projected increase therefore meant expansion both in terms of staff to cope with the anticipated greater numbers and in buildings to bring the premises up to date. By 1961 it was expected that a new dining room, kitchen, accommodation for physics, chemistry, general science, biology, rural science, art and crafts and two new gyms would be available. Two further women's halls of residence were also planned.

Preparations for the reception of male students were soon underway. By 1 September 1959 three men had been appointed to the staff: John E. Wilde, lecturer in PE, T.W. Eason, senior lecturer in education and A. Dawson, lecturer in physics. Stanley was to be the men's hall of residence.

The following table illustrates the upward spiralling of projected numbers:

| Date | Number (projected) |
|------|--------------------|
| 29.10.57 | 260 |
| 19.06.58 | 400 |
| 23.10.58 | 480 |
| 14.07.59 | 500 |
| 11.03.60 | 550 (suggested by the Ministry) |
| 19.03.63 | 660 |
| 01.11.63 | 750 (suggested by the Ministry) |

Within six years therefore Edge Hill was expected almost to triple.

The number of full-time and part-time staff showed an even greater increase:

| | |
|------|-----|
| 1956 | 26 |
| 1959 | 28 |
| 1961 | 37 |
| 1962 | 47 |
| 1963 | 59 |
| 1965 | 70 |
| 1965 (March) | 75 |
| 1966 | 96 |
| 1967 | 111 |

In 11 years staff had more than quadrupled; furthermore the dominance of men was quickly established. New appointments tended to be largely male: in September 1961, 13 out of 16 were men. From the initial three of 1959, by 1963 men made up 37 of the 57 full-time staff. And, though female students continued in the majority, female staff numbers declined rapidly: in 1966 there were 27 women to 66 men. The expansion actually meant a *reduction* of employment opportunities for women academics; a position which was reinforced with the appointment of the first male principal, Mr. P.K.C. Millins, a former HMI, to succeed Dr. Bain in Summer

**37**  *Princess Margaret opens new Halls of Residence, 1963.*

1964. (This was rather interesting since there appears no obvious reason, other than positive discrimination, why the introduction of a three-year course and the change to a mixed college should lead to such a transformation. Colleges which moved from being all-male to mixed were not inundated with women members of staff.)

Building developments proceeded slowly. By September 1962 the new gym was still not finished but was in use by the end of term. One of the main problems was lack of teaching space. The management had done very well to supply residential accommodation for 500 in single study bedrooms (a figure which hardly altered over the next quarter of a century); the rest either lived at home or in lodgings in Ormskirk.

The new extensions costing £500,000 and consisting of five women's halls, one for men, a double gym, dining rooms and extra science block were finally opened by Princess Margaret on 22 May 1963. The halls were named Lady Openshaw, Katharine Fletcher (after Chairmen of the Governors), E.M. Butterworth, Margaret Bain (after previous principals), and Eleanor Rathbone (a noted early 20th century social reformer and fighter for women's rights) and Lancashire.

The same period saw further, more radical changes being mooted on the academic front. In 1960 the National Advisory Council and Ministry of Education recommended a 'balance of training' policy. They assumed that the numbers of primary children would increase at 12.5 per cent but pupils at secondary schools would show only a slight rise. To cope with this students on college secondary courses were to be reduced from 37 per cent to 15 per cent and priority was to be given to maths and science (shortage subjects). This seemed to be relegating colleges to an inferior role, leaving them as the source of non-graduate teachers for infant and junior schools while the universities provided the graduate secondary teachers (as was the position in Scotland). Most colleges avoided this by bringing in 'junior-secondary' courses for the 9-13 age range. Edge Hill adopted a very sound compromise: the governors agreed to help by increasing the number of primary teachers and those who, though 'trained mainly for secondary work', could also teach in primaries 'without [the institution] committing itself to rigid proportions'.[3] In practice therefore, 'balance of training' did not markedly change the character of Edge Hill's secondary training.

Such rapid growth was obviously not achieved without difficulty and a new constitution was designed to cope. This gave all members of the Edge Hill community—domestic and maintenance staff as well as academics and students—the opportunity to serve on committees and provided for joint staff-student consultation machinery. It appeared to be working well: 'Potential areas of friction have already been eliminated or reduced through discussion and agreed action'.

Nevertheless, it was obvious that a lack of residential and teaching accommodation was not the only place where pressure was being felt. Mr. Millins identified two areas where resources were inadequate; there was a shortage of secretarial assistance which meant that tutors had to spend 'a disproportionate amount of time' doing routine clerical work; and the wardens were overburdened. To make their lot more tolerable it was proposed to improve their living conditions and appoint more assistant matrons to take over day-to-day administration (there were only three assistant domestic bursars for 650 students).[5] Despite this the transformation of Edge Hill from being an all-female, somewhat cosy little establishment into a large mixed institution had been achieved with relative ease.

# 7
# FROM ROBBINS TO JAMES TO INSECURITY

Nationally, however, the policy 'balance of training' did arouse fears. And, as a result, the Central Advisory Council with John Newsom as Chairman was asked in 1961 'to consider the education between the ages of thirteen and sixteen, of pupils of average or less than average ability ...' (i.e. those in secondary modern schools). Its report of August 1963—*Half Our Future*—proposed appropriate training for secondary modern teachers. Edge Hill quickly took up this challenge and by June 1965 Mr. Millins was able to report that one-term courses for 'teachers of "Newsom" children' were planned to take place between January to March and April to July 1966.

Newsom endorsed the effectiveness of colleges by maintaining that they should share in the training of graduate teachers and recommending that graduates should secure a professional qualification; in-service courses being provided for untrained graduates. Its belief in colleges led the Committee to request that its views be made known to the Robbins Committee on Higher Education which reported in October 1963.

This recommended: that training colleges be renamed college of education (quickly complied with because it cost nothing); that university links be strengthened by making university schools of education responsible for college government and finance; that a new B.Ed. degree should be operated by the Universities' Faculties of Education. Edge Hill therefore began offering the four year B.Ed. degree of Liverpool University from 1965. Strong local authority opposition to the second proposal, however, ensured that in 1965 the Government dropped it. Robbins also suggested a further dramatic increase in numbers: 1962-3 saw 49,000 students in 146 colleges. 1970-1 envisaged 82,000 in 156 with a minimum size of 750 (this would ensure sufficient resources and a wider range of staff for more specialised courses).

The continuing lack of teachers nevertheless led the National Advisory Council on the Supply and Training of Teachers to recommend, in June 1965, increased output from colleges from 1965-7. This was to be achieved by 'the more effective use of existing resources'; that is, no further expansion in the shape of new buildings. It included a scheme for a four-term year, a 'box and cox' arrangement of almost continuous teaching practice. It was felt that this would not overburden staff or prove detrimental to standards. The Wilson Government with its sights on its technological revolution accepted the recommendations and the DES published circular 7/65 (July 1965) which called for a 20 per cent increase in student numbers by utilising existing facilities more productively. Development plans were to be submitted by December 1965.

Already Edge Hill's expansion had been rapid. By January 1966 numbers were to reach 750 (including in-service students), which was to be achieved by means of new buildings ('as yet unstarted', reminiscent of Stalin's Five Year Plans' exploitation of yet undiscovered resources). According to Edge Hill's calculations, it would now be expected to take 985 with an annual intake of 328/9. If they also attracted 10 per cent B.Ed.s then there would be a total student population of 1,016 for *initial* training. It was not, however, proposed to rush into further expansion unless the minor adaptations to the teaching accommodation were carried out, since the postponement of the building programme till 1967 would place a severe strain on tutorial, kitchen and dining room provision. Therefore they did not propose to implement this suggested scheme till September 1967.[1]

If the alterations were made then Edge Hill would adopt a modified form of 'box and cox', i.e. half-year groups out of the institution for half a term at a time, while a whole-year group would be away for a term during the final teaching practice. This would necessitate an Edge Hill year of 36 weeks. With annual intakes of 328 this would give 956 students in September 1968, 1,014 by September 1969 (including 10 per cent fourth-year B.Ed.) and 1,016 by September 1970. This would have certain advantages: teaching practice would still be college-based, thus Edge Hill would keep control of professional training; professional and academic studies would receive equal attention; the B.Ed. courses would be related to University studies; it would promote stable community life; if the number of students living at home or in flats was raised to *c*.20 per cent the others could spend two years in residence; and students would still have a viable vacation period.[2] This seemed a much more realistic plan than, for example, the one proposed at Borough Road where a third of the students spent the term either on vacation or teaching practice. This naturally caused outrage from the Students Union.[3] There is no surviving evidence of any adverse reaction from Edge Hill Students Union. It was intended therefore that Edge Hill would play a full part in the DES expansion by 1970.

Even at the height of expansion, colleges were not immune from criticism. Professor Geoffrey Bantock in 1968 maintained that they neglected the academic side: 'My revolutionary suggestion is that students should be sent out, not only full of friendly feelings towards their charges, but actually *knowing* something. Even Facts. A profession defines itself, in part, in relation to the body of expertise which characterises its activities'.[4] A falling birth-rate also brought fears that colleges could no longer continue purely as teacher training institutions. The return of a Tory Government in June 1970 led to the appointment in December of the James Committee. Its brief was to examine and make recommendations (within 12 months) on all aspects of teacher education: content and organisation of courses; whether intending teachers should be educated separately from other students; and the respective roles of education colleges, polytechnics and universities.

The James Report, *Teacher Education and Training*, was published in January 1972. It recommended three 'Cycles' of teacher education: personal, pre-service and in-service training. In-service training was especially favoured and was to be expanded as a 'highest priority'. Colleges and polytechnics should offer new degree courses and a two-year Diploma in Higher Education (Dip.H.E.).

In the wake of this Report, Mr. Millins noted that 'The College is confident that it has an important part to play in Higher Education and that it can extend its already significant contribution to academic and professional studies both locally, regionally and, in some sectors, nationally too'.[5]

It responded positively to the 1972 Government White Paper: *Education: a framework for expansion*. This envisaged a new type of institution encompassing both teacher education and a wide range of B.A. degree courses. Since Edge Hill met the criteria necessary to be regarded as an institution specialising in the 'Arts and Human Sciences' and offering a 'reasonable range of advanced courses' for 1,000-2,000 students, it was hoped to expand to 1,500 students by 1979-80 and 1,800 by 1983-84 with equal numbers in teacher education and other categories of studies. To attract good quality students it aimed to offer degree courses (B.Ed. [Hons/Ord] and B.A. [Hons/Ord]) 'from the outset'. The two-year Diploma of Higher Education therefore in practice was to be relegated to the background; it might 'for the great majority of students, constitute Part I of a first degree, although it would be a terminal award in its own right for students unable or not wishing to proceed to a degree'.

To cope, an expansion of staff and buildings was required. [6] These included a professional centre, multi-purpose teaching blocks, 'both to replace the huts, built for five years in 1941, and to provide the extra lecture/seminar spaces needed'; Sports Hall 'to relieve the present almost intolerable strain on the gymnasia', Art/Craft centre, Drama Studio, staff tutorial accommodation, in service residential block, wardens' accommodation and students' centre. 'At present students' dances have to be held in the dining room: a most unhygienic arrangement.' Such were the heady days of the early 70s! By 1985, all that had been acquired was the in-service block through the accretion of Woodlands Chorley, a *non-residential* centre and some minor improvements to wardens' accommodation in the old halls. The huts were still in use, the gymnasia was still under pressure, staff shared rooms and students held dances in the dining room!

Validation was now proving a problem: after 24 years in the Liverpool Institute of Education, there was the possibility of a link with either CNAA or Lancaster University under its Associated Colleges policy. Edge Hill was obviously attracted to the latter, especially as, after local government reorganisation in 1974, it would remain within Lancashire while Liverpool became a part of Merseyside. Nevertheless they were 'very mindful of the many ties, over many years, of the College with Liverpool University, which we would not wish to alter lightly'. Caution and open-mindedness was counselled: 'It would be clearly irresponsible to attempt to make overtures to one validating body rather than another at a time when there are so many unknown factors. All the major avenues should be kept open. Close touch is being maintained with the College HMI, the Chief Education Officer and the Chairman of the Governors'. [7]

Lancaster's known flexibility towards its Colleges of Education, however, proved attractive, especially as its vice-chancellor (Charles Carter) and Professor A. Ross had developed the idea of a limited number of colleges undertaking a wide range of work including first degrees. It was therefore decided to take up Lancaster's offer and it became the validating body from September 1973, though Edge Hill would remain a member of the Liverpool Institute of Education for some of its functions as an Area Training Organisation, such as allocation of teaching practice places. [8]

For its part, Lancaster was aware that 'Edge Hill is a large and very strong college and the association would be a welcome one'. [9] It would help Lancaster, a new university, to build up strength in teacher education. In some ways this was almost a re-run of 1926 when Edge Hill had been taken over by Lancashire Education Committee. Once again therefore the institution was demonstrating its ability to adapt to altering circumstances and its willingness to meet these, rather than have change thrust upon it.

Three major B.A. degrees—Geography, English and Applied Social Sciences—were instituted in 1975. A further two—History and Combined Social Studies with a focus on Community Relations (later renamed Urban Policy and Race Relations)—followed shortly.

September 1975 saw the first completely *undergraduate* entry (i.e. intending students had to have a minimum of two 'A' levels). Obviously it was going to be more difficult to attract students since Edge Hill was now competing with universities and polytechnics. It was quite gratified therefore to have attracted 187 to the B.Ed. and 100 to the B.A. (a further 65 had been offered provisional places but had failed to secure the necessary two 'A' levels).

Examination of these students' origins shows once again the bias towards the North West. It was still particularly marked as far as the B.Ed.s were concerned; indeed if these people were considered within the old county boundaries then there was only a slight change from the late 19th early 20th centuries, i.e. 82 per cent coming from the North West, Yorkshire and Cumberland. The B.A.s reflected a slightly wider distribution, but even here 66 per cent came from the traditional catchment area.[10]

## TABLE XII

| Home Areas of First-Year Students | B.A. % of group | B.Ed. % of group |
|---|---|---|
| Merseyside | 18 | 18 |
| Greater Manchester | 9 | 10 |
| Southport/Ormskirk | 4 | 15 |
| Other parts of Lancashire | 27 | 29 |
| Yorkshire | 5 | 6 |
| Cumbria | 3 | 4 |
| North East | 6 | 2 |
| Midlands | 12 | 3-4 |
| South West and South East | 11 | 6 |

This level of recruitment was surpassed in 1976 when it was felt 'very satisfactory' to have recruited 296: 149 B.Ed. and 147 B.A. Over half the B.A.s and B.Ed.s were coming from Lancashire, Merseyside and Greater Manchester, though there appeared to have been a slight increase in the numbers coming from the South.

It was fortunate that B.A. recruitment was high, since national economic difficulties and a declining school population meant that the government required a major reduction in teacher training by 1981. The Director's Report for Easter 1977 announced that Edge Hill would receive '800 teacher education places ... the College will then have the largest number of teacher training places for a *single* institution in England and Wales'.

Diversification had been the challenge of the 1970s and by a mixture of good luck and good judgement Edge Hill had survived it. It had been careful to preserve its best traditions, among which was a commitment to voluntary work in the community. Under Mr. Millins' Directorship the full-time post of Community Work Organiser was established. Edge Hill had come a long way since the start of Mr. Millins' period of office. Mr. Millins, however, announced his wish to read for a higher degree at the end of the summer term 1978 and was given a sabbatical year prior to his resignation with effect from 31 August 1979. He was succeeded in the interim by the Deputy Director, Miss Marjorie W. Stantan, who had had a long association with Edge Hill. She was appointed Director. Dr. Brian Greaves who had been Assistant Principal of City of Liverpool College of HE became Deputy Director.

Miss Stantan had an awesome task in front of her. Colleges were in a vulnerable position. Given that resources for all higher education were limited they had to prove their case for

*38* *'Educational Cuts'*
*cartoon by B. Cook*

existence against the claims of the much stronger universities and polytechnics. In her Director's Report of Summer 1981 she reported that Edge Hill had borne cuts of a quarter of a million pounds in two years but had been enhanced by the acquisition of Preston Polytechnic's In-Service Teacher Education Unit at Woodlands. Thus 'The College is now administratively recognisable as an Advanced Further Education institution and looks forward to continued effort in academic and professional fields'. Such optimism was soon to be sorely tried in the shape of a threat of a merger with Preston Polytechnic. This aroused fears that such a merger would 'lead to a loss of University validation, to the transfer of courses to Preston and to the eventual closure of the Ormskirk campus, no matter what guarantees are currently given'. An all-out campaign was mounted and on 27 April 1982 Lancashire Education Committee passed a unanimous resolution that 'the merger be not proceeded with'. There was, however, to be a closer relationship between Edge Hill and Preston Polytechnic. 'These developments the College wholeheartedly supports now that its free-standing nature is accepted.'[11]

Miss Stantan had been Director for a relatively short time, yet she had faced and overcome immense problems. She had raised staff morale and, when she retired at the end of the Summer Term 1982, a fitting tribute came as Edge Hill was declared a 'centre of excellence' in teacher education in Autumn 1982. She was succeeded by Mr. Harry Webster who had held previous appointments at Ulster and Sunderland Polytechnics.

His directorate too was overshadowed by the constant threat of cuts. The National Advisory Body for Local Authority Higher Education (NAB) required Edge Hill to consider its position should it be faced with a 10 per cent reduction in financial resources between 1982 and 1984-5. An academic plan indicating the numbers of students which could be sustained without detriment to standards and the quality of education was submitted to NAB on 31 December 1982. This reaffirmed Edge Hill's intention to 'play its part in the national provision of higher education and to be particularly responsive to the plans of Lancashire County Council for its education service and to the needs of the local community and the north-west region'. In 1985 there were *c.*2,000 students on a wide variety of courses (B.A., B.Sc., B.Ed., M.A., Advanced Diploma and Certificate).

# 8
# TO INDEPENDENCE
# AND BEYOND

At the time of its centenary celebrations in 1985 it seemed that the best chance for Edge Hill's future success was to become a third force in higher education. Indeed, to quote from the first edition of this history:

> while successfully diversifying into general liberal arts degrees, it also promotes the attractions of a 'community college', hence its 'New Opportunities for Women' course, its 'Return to Study' course for mature students interested in entering higher education, its leisure courses such as photography. It is particularly interested in encouraging mature people to return to education and has therefore fostered various forms of access by developing a number of 'strong links and special links' with local Further Education Colleges. It continues its association with the North West Open College 'which enables mature students to prepare for entry to higher education' in local Further Education Colleges. Certain undergraduate lectures are open to the public under an 'Associate Students' scheme. This concentration on a wider system of higher education would seem to be Edge Hill's best chance of surviving into its next century.[1]

In the space of 11 years, however, the situation has proved very different. Edge Hill has became a University College with a student body of 6,500 on award-bearing courses, some 250 teaching staff and a wide range of diversified undergraduate and postgraduate provision in the Humanities and Arts, Management, Social Sciences, Science and Technology and Health Studies. The key to all this development was the Government white paper, *Higher Education— A Framework for Expansion*, published on 1 April 1987.

This proposed that colleges of HE with 55 per cent or more of their provision at HE level should, along with the polytechnics, no longer be under local authority control. They would become independent Higher Education Corporations with a new funding body—The Polytechnics and Colleges Funding Council (PCFC). This meant the creation of a new sector of HE which it was envisaged would take two years to achieve, coming into being on 1 April 1989. These new Higher Education Corporations would have boards of governors, on which representatives from business and industry would predominate. This was felt necessary since the corporations would own their own buildings and other assets. And in reflection of Thatcherite ideals, they would be competing in the market place. These proposals, which became enshrined in the 1988 Education Act, evoked mixed emotions. Generally polytechnics and colleges welcomed what they saw as freedom from local authority interference. Many at Edge Hill, however, took a different view. Lancashire had always been a very well-disposed local authority.

Independence therefore was seen as a great challenge and one to which the then management did not look forward. On the whole the institution felt very well served by Lancashire County Council. They had always been very supportive and the financial top-up they provided had become increasingly necessary, not to mention all the subsidiary services such as payroll, insurance, internal and external audit, cash investment and banking facilities, capital expenditure, programming and control, as well as establishment and personnel, property services, legal services, management information and co-ordinated purchasing. Edge Hill's administration was to be divided into five main areas, Finance, Registration, Buildings and Sites, Recruitment and Marketing, and Personnel. This would require additional staffing, such as an Academic Registrar, a Marketing Manager, Head of Personnel and their deputies and a Property Manager. Independence would mean that the institution would have to provide all these systems itself and would no longer have any cushioning. Edge Hill was now to be exposed to the market place with all that that entailed.

Equally, Edge Hill's connection with the University of Lancaster was seen as of considerable value. There was no general desire to go over to CNAA. Since 1975 (when Edge Hill had begun its connection with Lancaster University), it had developed three-year honours degrees, then higher degrees in the shape of taught M.A.s, and had taken a part in the validation process. The appointment of Dr. Brian Greaves (Deputy Director of Edge Hill), as the first non-university chairman of the Courses Committee (the committee that validated college courses), was evidence of the regard in which Edge Hill was held. Furthermore, it was believed that the connection with the University of Lancaster aided recruitment. Students received University of Lancaster degrees which were conferred on them at Lancaster University by the Chancellor, Princess Alexandra.

Edge Hill was fortunate in that its new Board of Governors, under the chairmanship of Mr. Bob Wilson, included the qualities needed to enable the institution to develop. Their task was massive: to transform an institution which had totally concentrated on the academic side of education into 'a self-contained, fully-fledged institution with complete autonomy, running its own affairs in terms of marketing, finance, personnel'.[2] This required a fundamental change in attitude and it took more than a year before the move towards business ideals and practices was fully appreciated among the Board of Governors. The Board, however, was always very supportive of Bob Wilson and prepared to trust his judgement.

All college assets were to be transferred to the new Higher Education Corporations. In some areas, where relations with the local council had not been good, a struggle ensued. Edge Hill again was fortunate. The main asset at issue was that of Woodlands, which had been an integral part of Edge Hill since 1981. It was not surprising, then, that the Board of Governors wished not only to retain its use but also to run it. Equally Lancashire County Council wanted it. To have pursued this 'battle' would have meant an extremely unproductive legal action, possibly lasting years, which the Governors rightly adjudged would be a waste of Edge Hill's funds. Careful negotiation secured Edge Hill the right to use Woodlands without charge, while Lancashire County Council retained ownership. This ensured that a fully operational in-service and conference centre was now available.

**39**  *Princess Alexandra meets the graduates.*

**40**  *Bob Wilson*

The process of independence might not have been one that Edge Hill would have voluntarily chosen but it passed through smoothly and the institution was well placed to meet the new challenges. It did not encounter a long bitter battle such as Luton had.[3]

Staff had been constantly reassured, however, that life would continue much as before and it was some time before there was a general realisation of what independence entailed. The process involved both restraints and challenges. There were fears about becoming enmeshed in an enterprise culture which was to cause problems when Ruth Gee attempted change,[4] but there was no doubt that independence brought new chances for expansion.

Each institution had now to produce a three-year strategic plan for further development and growth. Edge Hill had been accustomed to think in terms of development plans since 1984 and so was able to build on its previous strengths of high support to individual students. It saw itself as a 'medium size' institution and had no desire to try to compete with, for example, Lancashire Polytechnic in areas where polytechnics had always been strong—hard science and engineering. Rather it sought to enhance its strengths in the liberal arts, while at the same time branching out into business and information technology.

Effective management was now even more vital. Throughout the 1980s Edge Hill underwent a period of consolidation characterised by much sound day-to-day administration. Access to higher education had been increased through growing numbers of mature students (over 21). By the mid-1980s they represented 35 per cent of the intake (including in-service students). This was in direct contrast to the 'old' universities where 'matures' averaged around 10 per cent. Such change, however, was no longer sufficient to meet the challenges of the 1990s, and the Board of Governors therefore charged the new director (Ruth Gee) with a brief to develop Edge Hill, ensuring that it caught up rapidly with others in the sector.

# 9
# GROWTH AND DIVERSITY

Ruth Gee was, on her own admission, an unusual choice for director. She had had little experience of higher education, having spent most of her career teaching in secondary schools, though she was deputy leader of the Inner London Education Authority from 1983 to 1986 and then Assistant Director of North London Polytechnic, 1986-9.[1] Nevertheless she was to take over in a period in which she oversaw and promoted massive change. That change was necessary is now in no doubt—expand or perish—but the scale and type of change caused conflict and tension amongst the staff. Nationally, higher education was now expected to reflect and respond to the needs of the market economy; this meant a move away from what many saw as the natural traditions of academe to the introduction of business management and accountability. Decisions had to be made quickly; it was now no longer possible to wait 18 months for a consensus to emerge.

Edge Hill, however, had always seen as one of its strength, its human face with its care for the individual student. Many staff feared that this would go with rapidly expanding numbers and what was seen as new alien demands (such as appraisal) being put on staff. Ruth Gee had made it clear from her very first staff meeting that in her view massive change was necessary. She was in no doubt that Edge Hill had to carve its own niche, using its traditions and strengths to differentiate it from its competitors. She wanted to retain its distinctiveness, but this meant a clear vision of what this entailed: how courses differed and how they were provided. The future was not about being third rate but about being different.

For successful change to take place certain factors must be present. Ruth Gee, however, was perhaps unfortunate in that staff had to some extent been shielded from the realities of life. A culture of embracing change was certainly not evident. A document issued by Harry Webster, 'The Education Act 1988: Statement of Progress' stated:

> The fundamental principle underlying the changes in the Education Act of 1988 which will affect Edge Hill College appears to be that we should be more like a business, being subjected to market forces and able to respond creatively to them. The results are intended to be increased value for the public money involved and increased effectiveness in meeting the demands and needs of our society and especially of its economy. To achieve these results, the most significant changes are being made in the government of the system and of its institutions and in the financing of the system. These changes are characterised by a combination of increased central control and increased institutional independence … Both, of course, have been achieved by eliminating LEA control of all institutions which are predominantly concerned with higher education.[2]

Such ambivalence towards change was widespread. As Ruth Gee stated, 'creating a vision owned and shared by the majority is essential in all organisations and higher education is no exception … Although I shared (and still do) the staff's sense of a need for local and open accountability, their hope was that things would go away. How could I generate a sense of reality and from that a shared vision?'[3] To achieve this *all* staff, in whatever capacity, had to realise that her/his contribution was vital to the success of the institution (that is, the concept of total quality management was being introduced *without* the formal structures). The Chief Executive and the Governors had been concerned to bring Edge Hill's management structures up to date so that they did not restrict and inhibit progress. The balance of provision within the institution now lay with Humanities and Social Sciences but power still lay with the Education faculties, reflecting Edge Hill's former role as a training college. The three faculties were disbanded therefore, as a prelude to the introduction of learning areas, which in turn would be grouped into Schools.

Diversity in provision was obviously important. There was no desire to down-grade or weaken teacher education. The aim was to diversify and grow, building on previous developments. The *Updated Strategic Plan to 1992* detailed these: a bold initiative in the shape of a B.Sc. in Organization and Management Studies had been achieved without PCFC funding, relying instead on income from student fees and the use of existing staff; a B.Sc. in Field Biology & Habitat Management indicated Edge Hill's interest in the environment; B.A.s in English and French, Modern European Studies, Communications and Information Media, part-time M.A.s in Writing Studies, History, Human Rights and Equal Opportunities as well as a B.Ed. in Business Education had also taken place. Another exciting development concerned the setting up of the Project 2000 Diploma in Nurse Education.[4]

The Board of Governors, Chief Executive and Senior Management Team correctly assessed external pressures which were producing challenges to traditional assumptions and values. Funding was clearly linked to size; therefore teaching group size had to increase which meant that teaching methods must change. Andrew Sackville was appointed to a new senior position, Head of Teaching and Learning Development, to pioneer new ways of teaching and learning. He aimed to provide a co-ordinated range of services to improve existing methods. This would entail using available resources more effectively and ensuring that the learning experience did not suffer because of increased student numbers. Students were to be supported not only by staff and tutors on their programme, but also by a range of staff in learning support areas across the institution. In December 1994 the Academic Board adopted a College Teaching and Learning Policy. A Teaching and Learning Development Fund was also established to support projects from the subject areas. The results of these projects are disseminated through the publication TALEX (Teaching and Learning Exchange) which comes out once a term and the 'Action Learning Network', a cross-institution staff development group. A fortnightly newsletter TALIS (Teaching and Learning Information Sheet) gives staff information about teaching and learning developments. This was a timely initiative since student numbers increased much quicker than expected with all the consequent needs for support that these brought. ASSIST has proved very helpful here.

ASSIST is an acronym for 'Access for Students and Staff to Information Services and Technology'. It encompasses support for teaching and learning in the areas of Computer Services, Library Services, Mediatech Services and Teaching and Learning Development and was launched in September 1993. It now has a customer base of 7,000 people since it provides services not just for students but also for teaching and support staff. It promotes staff development for new staff and a postgraduate certificate in Teaching and Learning Support in Higher Education. A Student Learning Support Officer provides drop-in skill sessions for students as well as support for students with dyslexia and learning difficulties. It has been successfully externally evaluated by the HEQC Audit of January 1996 and by every HEFCE subject assessment. One of its problems is its continued success, since this raises expectations of what can be provided. Nevertheless, it is a highly valued part of the support mechanisms.

In addition Ruth Gee saw the need for the use of IT. The provision of IT is now seen as commonplace, but in 1989/90 a decision to go for a technological infrastructure was a major development departure. Edge Hill had displayed an interest in computers since 1970 when Dr. Roy Morgan of the Mathematics Department had introduced an Olivetti terminal which was linked via a modem to Preston Polytechnic (now the University of Central Lancashire) and used for data processing. Computing at this stage relied heavily on the enthusiasm of individuals. Dr. Morgan wrote his own programmes to teach maths to teacher training students and Edge Hill was one of the first institutions in Britain in the early 1970s to provide computer studies for its student teachers. Later, in the early 1980s, Dr. Dunn and Mr. Malcolm Hind, also lecturers in the maths department, pioneered further work: Dr. Dunn with research machines and Malcolm Hind with his computer work for handicapped children. Computers, however, were beginning to assume a higher profile as the 1980s progressed. They were now an important tool in the administration. In 1985 Macintoshes were introduced, along with a small number of PCs. There was, however, still no policy to bring computing facilities to the institution as a whole.[5]

Ruth Gee decided that every course was to have an IT component and students were to be given this as an entitlement. IT was seen as a transferable skill which would be of great use

**41**   *New technology in the music studio*

**42**   *Computer facilities in the Learning Resource Centre*

in a student's future career. Accordingly, by September 1993, Edge Hill had signed a million-pound partnership deal with the leading computer company, ICL. This contract ensured state of the art facilities for staff and students and meant a further improvement in the students' overall learning experience. The ratio of student to computer improved from 11:l to 6:l, meaning that Edge Hill had one of the highest provisions in the country.

The Governors and the Chief Executive were also aware that marketing was now to be of paramount importance. A marketing and communications office, an access and equal opportunities unit, as well as a discrete personnel unit and a more effective finance office were quickly established. The 1992/3 to 1995/6 development plan demonstrated how the institution was growing in confidence and self assurance: better marketing was immediately evident. The mission statement was much sharper. It boldly stated:

> Edge Hill … is firmly committed to meeting the needs of students, the region and its economy, through its role as education provider, employer and community resource. It recognises that its strength and continuous growth lies in its proven ability to anticipate and respond to its needs. [Edge Hill] intends to build on its strengths as it reaches the optimum size to sustain a cost-effective, supportive, campus-based institution.

The 'watchwords for the conduct of College affairs' were to be 'honesty, openness and trust'.

Great stress was laid on equal opportunities which were 'to permeate all aspects of the curriculum and life generally', staff development (staff had to 'spend up to six days planning and

reviewing academic related matters') and the gender and ethnic balance. Here it was pointed out that though three of the five members of the Directorate were women, this did not reflect the position in the institution as a whole; 'although many capable women exist within the College they are not represented in equal numbers at Head of Learning or Head of Service level'.[6] Equally the lack of staff from black and ethnic groupings caused concern, and therefore the mission statement committed the institution to 'work to increase access and opportunity for members of under-represented groups'.[7]

Edge Hill must also be in a position to compete effectively in the new environment. This meant sound policies for recruitment and the introduction of modularisation. A policy of developing strong links with a selected group of further education colleges was adopted. This paid dividends in attracting students, though the worry now is that it represents too small a base. Coming relatively late to modularisation, Edge Hill felt itself in a position to develop the best possible practices. Once again, however, many staff remained to be convinced of its benefits. There were fears that it would involve the academic equivalent of 'pick and mix', with students picking and choosing modules from whatever subjects they fancied. In practice, though courses were opened up and new subjects such as Women's Studies and Sports Studies came on stream, students tended to stick to traditional pathways. Modularisation has worked well; it has the benefit of allowing students to progress at a variable pace and to change from full-time to part-time as needed. It also meant that various kinds of prior learning can be used as entry qualifications or part of a degree award. Edge Hill invested much money in its systems and from September 1993 courses were modularised.

## I Equal Opportunities

Despite the fact that Edge Hill had begun life as a Women's Training College, by the late 1970s it had taken on a distinct masculine face as regards its management practices; Ruth Gee was quick to appreciate this. Development of effective Equal Opportunities policies was taken very seriously and Equal Opportunities quickly became a cornerstone of Edge Hill's new image. The institution was not afraid to state that it lacked systematic information on the experience and position of women as a group; the extent and consequences of homophobia and heterosexism on different groups (young women, older women, anti-sexist men); and the ways in which lesbian and gay students might find the Edge Hill environment unwelcoming, alienating or threatening. An Access and Equal Opportunities Audit of social class, employment status, gender, age, race, sexual preference, ability/disability was also to be undertaken. Equal Opportunities criteria were to become part of the process of course evaluation and access strategies. The desire was to create a fairer environment for all and to banish student activities such as degrading initiation ceremonies and slave auctions. The result was draft Equal Opportunities policies covering the three main areas of employment, education and the curriculum and community provision, paying particular attention to race, colour, ethnicity, gender, age, disability and sexual orientation. These quickly became policy.

There was no doubt that the ideas of Equal Opportunities permeating all aspects took time, particularly with regard to course content. Nevertheless the Equal Opportunities policies were an important aspect of attempts to create a quality culture stressing the values of honesty, trust, respect and empowerment. Further projects were soon underway, such as APTAB (later renamed the Lancashire Project) and, more recently, a Widening Access Project. APTAB stood for Access to Primary Teaching for Asians and Black People, and was the result of co-operation between Edge Hill, S. Martin's College, Lancaster University and Lancashire County Council. Its aim was to bring more people from black and ethnic groupings into teaching. As only 2.5 per cent of teachers were from these groups, they were grossly underrepresented in the primary classroom, particularly in Lancashire where, out of 5,000 primary teachers, only seven were from ethnic groupings. It was designed to overcome some of the difficulties which these students might have in attending an institution some distance from their homes, by operating the majority of the degree programme from East Lancashire. Students took the first part of their degree at a local college—Accrington & Rossendale, Blackburn, Burnley, Nelson & Colne, and Preston, their professional work at a specially developed Professional Centre in Blackburn, and then might attend either Edge Hill or S. Martin's for their subject work.

The Widening Access Project aims to encourage greater participation in higher education by under-represented groups in selected areas of Lancashire and Merseyside—those with disabilities, women returners and black and other ethnic groupings. Partnerships have been developed with a range of organisations. Targeted groups have attended open days, visits have been made to schools and colleges to discuss opportunities and short courses have been put on as 'tasters'.

In 1996 Edge Hill has also successfully attracted HEFC funding of £164,455 over three years 'to encourage High Quality Provision for students with Specific Learning Difficulties'. This will be used to help establish and evaluate a Specific Provision Centre for students with learning difficulties and disabilities; to increase the number of disabled students in higher education and enhance their learning experiences by exploiting alternative media and IT formats; to widen the resource base of staff who can work with students with disabilities and to network this model with all interested parties. This again is evidence of the fact that Edge Hill takes Equal Opportunities seriously and is not prepared to rest on its laurels but is constantly trying to make the Edge Hill learning experience fit the requirements of and to stretch those with disabilities. Its desire is to increase access and secure admission of those from under-represented groups, matures, those from ethnic grouping and those with disabilities.

## II Health Studies

After two years of fruitful negotiations undertaken on behalf of the institution by Dr. John Cater, a new partnership was developed with the Sefton School of Health Studies. On 2 May 1990 the University of Lancaster and the English National Board for Nursing, Midwifery and Health Visiting jointly validated the Diploma of Higher Education/Registered Nurse Practitioner in Nursing Studies. This was to lead, in October 1990, to the successful beginnings of Nurse Education at Edge Hill in the shape of a Project 2000 course. Project 2000 was designed to improve the academic standards of nurses by producing a course backed by both the English National Board for Nursing and a College of Higher Education (in this case, Edge Hill). Initial approval was given for five years. On successful completion of the course, students would receive a Diploma in Higher Education (Nursing Studies) as well as a professional qualification.

*43    School of health studies*

*44    Health studies*

This gave nursing students the chance to mix with other higher education students, thereby increasing their educational experience. Students would spend their first 16 weeks at Edge Hill studying a foundation course which would be followed by a developmental programme over 14 months, covering health and related subjects. Their second 18 months would be taken up with specialising in Adult Mental Handicapped or Mental Health Nursing, the idea being to extend the range of non-institutional experience in the local community while at the same time ensuring their time on the wards would be educationally led.

This was a very important development for Edge Hill: it was an attempt to diversify from what was now seen as a rather narrow base; to provide community and vocational training to increase the size of the institution and to provide a new source of funding not dependent on PCFC, though of course this was somewhat precarious in that it was not

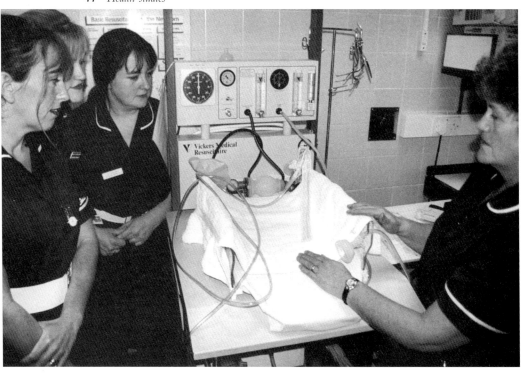

*guaranteed* income. Once again it was hoped that it would recruit among those not traditionally a part of higher education and even have the possibility of appealing to the overseas market. This proved to be a very successful partnership and in 1993 led to formal incorporation of the Sefton School of Health Studies into Edge Hill. This was organised jointly by Edge Hill and the Mersey Regional Health Authority and gave 650 trainee nurses full access to campus facilities.

In early 1994 a multi-million pound deal between Mersey Regional Health Authority and Edge Hill was signed to safeguard the future of nurse training. The contract was worth £11 million over five years. Edge Hill was now a major provider of nurse and midwifery education and training at both the Ormskirk site and Fazakerley (Aintree Hospital). Its pre- and post-registration courses were validated by Lancaster University and the English National Board for Nursing, Midwifery and Health Visiting. Fifty per cent of the pre-registration course was spent on work placements. By 1995 pre-registration courses included: Project 2000 (with branches in adult, mental health, learning disabilities and children's nursing) and midwifery, while post-registration encompassed a range of specialisms such as Accident and Emergency and intensive/coronary care nursing. Also offered was a Dip.H.E. in Health Studies and a Dip.H.E. in Counselling, a B.Sc. (Hons) Health Studies, a B.Sc. (Hons) in Health Care Practice and a B.Phil.

The English National Board gave an unconditional five years' approval (the maximum which could be given) to these courses. The ENB also gave the School of Health Studies authority to self-validate courses, a form of recognition given to only a few institutions.

As well as promoting undergraduate study, Edge Hill University College is also actively involved in researching health care and health related issues. The Centre for Health Research and Evaluation (CHRE) under the direction of its founder, Dr. Tom Chapman, deputy head of Health Studies, has undertaken several large research projects from local health authorities. Research interests include a study of the health and social care needs of the Formby elderly (undertaken jointly with Alan Johnson of Applied Social Sciences); Asian women and the health service; an assessment of home rehabilitation for hip surgery patients; evaluation of community treatment of leg ulcers; development of clinical guidelines for breast cancer patients; and patient empowerment. Dr. Chapman is keen to emphasise that the Centre should reflect the opinions of the users: 'Many of the recent changes in the NHS have been aimed at reducing costs and making efficiency savings.

**45** *New entrance to the main building*

*46*   *Student accommodation*

We need to ensure that the voice of the customer is not lost in the pursuit of economic rationalisation.'[8] As well as providing a service for the community, the CHRE has been instrumental in raising Edge Hill's profile as a research institution.

The School of Health Studies has become a highly respected and valued part of Edge Hill's provision. Over sixty academic and twenty-five support staff provide teaching and development. Its importance lies in the variety of diploma and degree level modules and pathways available to meet the requirements for practitioners in all specialisms. It was the first institution in the country to have a maxilo-facial course. Its flexible programmes offer several potential pathways so that second-level practitioners can convert to become first-level. Wherever possible it attempts to meet the needs of students in a flexible way and to further Edge Hill's commitment to widening access by providing twilight classes. The school works closely with a number of National Health Trusts, as well as the voluntary and private health care sector, and social services. In addition, it provides counselling for a number of organisations. Well-developed links with the Liverpool Marie Curie Centre mean that highly-regarded modules on cancer care are available.

# 10
# DEVELOPMENT OF THE FABRIC

Not only was the institution growing, its fabric also had to increase commensurately. To create a modern, up-to-date image, it was necessary to upgrade the buildings. Extensive refurbishments were undertaken. These included a new entrance and reception area (which some rather unkindly compared to that of a modern supermarket), the complete refurbishment of teaching rooms on the first floor of the main building, so that they met the highest standards with built-in audio and video capabilities, and a graphics studio in the Craft, Design and Technology building. In line with the mission statement, disabled access to the main building was improved and rooms in Lady Margaret Hall were converted to provide a purpose-built flatlet for a disabled student and carer.

Expansion carried on apace, and with imaginative management new capital projects got off the ground. A new student accommodation complex, Forest Court, was built on the former

**47**   *Forest Court*

*48*   *Natural and applied sciences*

*49*   *Sages*

football pitch adjacent to St Helens Road at a cost of £3.25m. The three-storey building provided 300 student resident places, half of the rooms having en-suite facilities. Computer terminal points were also provided in the rooms to enable students to log onto Edge Hill's network. Further new buildings included the new Maths block behind the Levens, and the Natural & Applied Science building (cost £1.5m), handed over in 1995, which was equipped with several specialist laboratories as well as a lecture theatre, research areas and preparation and seminar rooms.

The next phase of Edge Hill's ongoing refurbishment encompassed a new student block on the site of the old refectory. This would house a bar, lounge, dance floor, fast-food outlet, a games room and a launderette. *Sages* dining room was to be refurbished and relocated in what had been in 1933 the original dining room but which had since been used as the education resource centre. It would provide dining facilities for one hundred and fifty. To cater for the increasing numbers of students, the Terrace Café was expanded by creating a new mezzanine area. This allowed seating for 320 people. These developments have been very successful in providing on-campus facilities for students.

## I Learning Resource Centre and Student Information Centre

Edge Hill was also very fortunate in having an extremely go-ahead Head of Library Services, Ruth Jenkinson, who with her team was ready to take advantage of the new technological age. Ruth had joined Edge Hill in 1981 from Crewe & Alsager College. She became Acting Edge

**50** *The Learning Resource Centre*

Hill Librarian in 1983, a position which was confirmed in 1984. At that time the library held
80,000 volumes, 140 study spaces and 500 journal titles.

With the backing of Ruth Gee who herself was very interested in the concept of a
*Learning* Resource Centre, i.e. an area where a student could do all his/her learning with access
to knowledge in all its forms, a start was made on plans for a new centre. The possibility of
extending the existing library was considered and rejected. A new building which could house
both IT and a traditional library seemed the best solution. Edge Hill did not feel that the two
activities could co-exist since IT users liked to chat to each other while readers preferred quiet.
It was also realised that students would need a lot of support and help if they were to get the
most out of the new system, so a Help Desk which has proved invaluable was provided. *ASSIST*
also produced many helpful leaflets.

This was another major capital project—£2.8m—of which major funding (40 per cent)
came from HEFC. At the ceremony to lay the foundation stone, Tim Boswell, minister for
Further & Higher Education, saw the building as being an 'important investment in students'
careers. For some years, Edge Hill has put into practice national policies locally, particularly the
government's commitment to access. As participation in higher education remains high many
students will benefit from the centre. The experience and qualifications they gain will allow
them to earn and enjoy their place in a changing world.'

The new building (opened on 31 January 1994) was up and running within 38 weeks.
This was a tremendous achievement; not only was the building ready on time, all stock moved,

but library staff had been trained to help students to use the new materials and resources. Overnight the 'library' had changed from 10 PCs on a local network to a state of the art 'Learning Resource Centre' with 150 PCs, totally networked, including 50 multi-media workstations. The LRC could hold 250,000 items in open access with a further 40,000 available in closed storage. The building was officially opened by the Chief Executive of HEFCE, Professor Graeme Davies, who paid tribute to Edge Hill's 'obvious commitment to excellence in higher education', noting the 'star quality' of its staff and students.

The LRC has gone from strength to strength. The provision of CD ROMs, inter-library loans and periodicals continues to grow, while the percentage spent on books is declining. There is an increasing demand for electronic information sources. The World Wide Web is extremely popular and LRC staff have been finding useful Web sites which are then shared with other librarians. Frontiers are constantly being pushed forwards: there are 30 modem links into partner schools so that student teachers can access library catalogues and e-mail Edge Hill University College. One hall of residence is fully networked. The LRC sees itself as a gateway to resources. Already it is looking at the question of telephone support. The LRC provides a service which is both flexible and proactive, designed to provide the best opportunities to enhance student learning experience.

The LRC has become more and more directly involved in the teaching and learning process, enabling students to do more directed independent study. The number of students has tripled during Ruth Jenkinson's time but the number of staff has shown very little increase. Electronic improvement has helped, but at the end of the day students still expect a human being to be on hand to deal with problems/ enquiries. In recognition of this, Help Desks are available, staffed by highly trained assistants

*51    The Learning Resource Centre*

*52    Student Information Centre*

who are able to provide immediate help on problems connected to library services and computing services. Students are also given the opportunity to develop a wide range of IT skills. Workshops, drop-ins, and other practical sessions are offered by staff while specialist IT skills are provided by Computer Services. These are extremely popular and ensure that the student is well-equipped to undertake fully independent learning.

Given all this, it is not surprising to find that an Independent Review by Touche Ross revealed that Edge Hill University College was in the top 10 per cent of spenders (omitting the 'old universities') and this reflected the level of commitment to learning resources.

|  | EHUC | New Universities |
|---|---|---|
| Total space per FTE student (sq m) | 1.47 | 0.58 |
| FTE students per seat | 6.13 | 10.15 |
| Shelving per FTE student (ft) | 2.52 | 1.07 |
| Study hours per FTE student | 10.18 | 6.35 |
| Total books per FTE student | 51.8 | 29.8 |
| Total periodical titles per FTE student | 0.27 | 0.23 |
| Volumes of books in stock/FTE library staff numbers | 7491 | 5034 |
| Documents delivered per FTE student | 91.1 | 44.8 |
| Total loans per volume in stock | 1.76 | 1.56 |
| Total items processed /FTE library staff | 709.61 | 309.81 |
| FTE students per member of professional library staff | 330.0 | 421.3 |
| Documents delivered/FTE library staff numbers | 13,184 | 10,070 |
| Total expenditure per FTE student | 184.00 | 173.37[1] |

The provision of a new central purpose-built library also meant that the 'old library' was now available. This became the new Student Information Centre, a one-stop building where students could find help on all aspects of their courses as well as assistance with more general and perhaps personal problems. Registry, Office of Modular Programmes and Assessment, Careers, Teaching and Learning Support, Student Services and Computer Services are housed in the SIC, as well as new open-access computer facilities.

The Student Information Centre is part of Edge Hill's attempt to ensure a student support infrastructure which empowers students, enabling them 'to support themselves and to acquire skills for the future at the same time as getting the support they need during their university experience'.[2] The feeling that this should exist was reinforced by HEFCE funding criteria which called for quality support networks for students to enable them to achieve their full potential.

Accordingly, in 1991, Sue Aldridge was appointed Head of Student Services, a senior management position, to provide a viable student services support structure. This was a vast undertaking involving not just student discipline and halls management but also accommodation, children, counselling and health services. Sue produced a three-year development plan to initiate the desired changes. It was felt that the existing system of Hall Wardens and Hall Presidents worked against equal opportunities and promoted the worst features of a public-school ethos. Wardens became Residential Advisors who now worked in concert with Student Assistants who were fully trained in equal opportunities (through a two-day compulsory session). Training now includes mediation and conflict resolution which has proved invaluable in resolving disputes in Halls.

**53**  *Computer facilities*

Sue was also keen to improve facilities for the non-resident students who now accounted for 75 per cent of the total student body. Child-care was of particular importance here and the development of nursery education at Westend Primary School in Ormskirk has been much appreciated, though there are not always enough crèche places to go round at times of peak demand. Twenty places are provided: four for two year olds and 16 for three to five year olds. Children have to be two to come, which militates against those with very young children. Cost, though on a sliding scale, is still often prohibitive. A refurbished Derby Hall (the centre for non-resident students) was also provided.

All in all, Student Services have proved to be a great success. Workshops are provided on house-hunting and finance, the accommodation list is available on the computer network and a well-used comprehensive counselling service with open days is available. Counselling provides a much valued support system not simply in crisis situations but also as a means of promoting self-development groups which offer a safe haven for students to talk through their experiences. Counselling sessions have increased from 12 sessions in 1991 to 32 in 1996 and are available at times designed to enable students to attend. A Welfare Rights Officer also provides advice and support for students on all aspects of welfare rights and financial management. Particular support is given by the Welfare Rights Officer to students with disabilities or particular cultural needs both before they come to Edge Hill, and during their course. The 1996 HEQC Quality Audit commented, 'the team would wish to commend the particularly active approach of the Library, Student Services and the Careers Services in supporting students'.[3] Students have also had a significant role in producing a *Student Charter* with an associated *Complaints Procedure*.

This is vital given the ever-increasing number of students and the declining unit of resource and contributes to the fact that Edge Hill has a very high retention rate. This change in attitude since 1990 again represents the move to a more self-confident, mature culture, instead of one which provided purely supportive pastoral services aiming to replicate a parents' responsibility for children.

Ruth Gee left Edge Hill on 1 September 1993 to take up a new post in Further Education as Chief Executive of the Association of Colleges. She had overseen Edge Hill through a very challenging time and had certainly done much to raise its profile, leaving the institution in a much stronger position than when she had come. Working with the Board of Governors and the Senior Management Group, funding had been secured for the LRC and refurbishing the new entrance and the top corridor in the main building, while a bank loan had been acquired for Forest Court. Student numbers had doubled and there had been a dramatic increase in the number of courses available. Ruth's strengths had been in her vision; her ability to see what would be needed over the next decade and in her determination to let nothing stand in her way. She at times made unpopular decisions and was not afraid to be forceful, leading from the front, which, as she realised, did make her enemies.[4] There can be no doubt, however, that her period as Chief Executive contributed significantly to Edge Hill's development as an independent institution. She had made Edge Hill realise that it had to change and by her energy ensured that it did.

## II  The Grounds

One of Edge Hill's greatest boons since moving to Ormskirk has been its extensive grounds. And despite the recent building developments, the essential character has remained. Much of the credit for the gardens belongs to Mary Coles who was a gardening student from 1933/34 and then appointed Lecturer in Gardening in 1949. It is impossible to describe all the aspects of the grounds but certain 'landmarks' are of particular interest. When the new site was commissioned for Edge Hill there were only three trees on its 45 acres and up to its opening in 1933 the only planting that had been done was that of some young lime trees along the main drive and the Ruff Lane entrance. The Rock Garden and the Rose Garden did not exist except in imagination. This gives some idea of the magnitude of the task facing staff and students. A start was made by planting roses at the front of the institution and 20 years later many of the originals were still in bloom. Vegetables from the Kitchen Garden were available in 1934.

The Rock Garden was started in the winter of 1934/35 and completed in 1936 when the Rose Garden was begun, though it was to be 1937 before it really took shape. By the time of the outbreak of war in 1939, then, much had been achieved. For the next seven years, however, Edge Hill was at Bingley and the grounds as well as the buildings were requisitioned for the war effort. This meant that not only were the ornamental parts of the grounds neglected but the front lawns were ploughed up for vegetables. Return to peace-time therefore occasioned much work. Happily the Rose Garden had not suffered too badly and by 1948 was restored to much of its former glory. The Rock Garden had not fared so well: weeds had completely overrun it and as late as 1953 they still had the upper hand, so that it had to be replanted.

It was during the post-war period that a great deal of attention was given to tree planting. This was an area in which Mary Coles excelled. Her interest was in trees which had 'teaching

**54**   *The grounds*

potential' as well as individual merit and contributed to the overall landscape. Dr. Margaret Bain gave a grove of birch trees and 'John Downie' crab apple trees replaced the limes (which had never really taken) along the front drive.

As a result of Mary's effort many interesting, unusual trees remain to interest today's students; ginkgo or maidenhair trees, Atlantic Cedar, Scots and Corsican pines, a Robena or locust tree, while those in the Rock Garden are fine examples of contrasting colour and growth forms. An excellent description of this is given by Bob Slatter, former Senior Lecturer in Biology:

> The island bed on the right contains a deodar cedar, native to the Himalayas. At this point you are encircled by unusual conifers—noble fir, red cedar, western hemlock, Japanese cedar, and a small deciduous down redwood. On the west side of the rock garden are the beech, red oak, Lambeam, plane ash, sycamore and a tulip tree with its curiously shaped leaves and aromatic bark. No longer

native, this species was known to grow in the Thames Valley some 50m years ago when the climate was several degrees warmer.[5]

As a fitting tribute to Mary Coles, the old Arts and Science building is to be named 'The Mary Coles Building'.

In Mary Coles' days, 10 groundsmen and gardeners were employed. Today a team of four under the leadership of Head Gardener, Derek Sumner, maintain the 70-acre site. This is a 365 days a year job. Every plant on campus has been grown in Edge Hill's greenhouses. The institution no longer grows its own produce—an expertly planned arboretum replaces the once cultivated area. As Derek Sumner says: 'Gardening is all about bringing out the best in things. It's about adapting to the times and money with them'.[6] Not only does the Gardening Team bring great pleasure to all who use the campus, they also provide facilities for the Field Biology and Habitat Management department by developing a new border specially designed to attract butterflies.

## III  Woodlands

Woodlands, situated on the outskirts of Chorley, 17 miles from Ormskirk, provides an In Service and Conference Centre for Edge Hill. The majority of Edge Hill's Professional and Continuing Education takes place here with a wide variety of courses on offer: postgraduate diplomas in counselling, careers and related studies, in early years, in special education needs, post graduate certificate, diploma, M.A. and M.Phil. in education management; B.A. in education and community studies, M.A. in educational studies, as well as B.Phil. by research and a number of other in-service programmes.

Also situated at Woodlands is the Mentoring Centre (to provide a forum in which colleagues can share and explore the practice of mentoring) and the National Primary Centre. Since 1991 Edge Hill has been the North West regional base for the National Primary Centre which works to develop links between headteachers, teachers in higher education institutions and local authorities.

# 11
# THE WIDER COMMUNITY

Edge Hill has always been conscious of its responsibilities to the wider community. It wants to share its privileges and advantages, hence its desire to promote cultural developments, its opening of the new Sports Complex to the region as a whole, as well as its educational and other partnership links.

## 1 Cultural Developments

**55** *Promoting cultural development*

Edge Hill was concerned to develop the physical environment as a culture centre. April 1989 saw the beginnings of the sculpture park (the brainchild of Peter Oakley), when Edge Hill secured eight sculptures on a long-term loan. By March 1990, 12 sculptures were on show, all by north-west sculptors: Ted Roocroft, Robert Scriven, Philip Bews, Christine Kowal Post and Marjorie Wouda. The aim was to make a positive contribution to the Arts in West Lancashire by giving sculptors an opportunity to display their work in an outdoor setting, something which was rare in Lancashire, and to provide a major artistic attraction in line with the policy of opening the institution to the community since all sculptures were to be accessible to the disabled. The collection grew quickly, encompassing work by both professional and student artists in a wide variety of media—wood, steel, stone, cold cast resin. Only a few of the many sculptures can be described here (where possible the sculptors' own words are used).

*56*   *The Eternal Struggle*

*Bingo Bango* (constructed in 1981) by Robert Scriven is situated on the front lawn. The breakdown of relationships was the inspiration for the sculpture made from welded steel. Its intricate construction means that shadows are cast and at intervals the shadows of the two figures actually meet, emphasising the loneliness of the couple. To quote Scriven,

> I conceived this piece while the disintegration of personal relationships was happening. Had the outcome been different then so would the sculpture. The title is from a line by F Scott-Fitzgerald and works better than 'Here today—Gone tomorrow'.

*The Eternal Struggle* by Dan Manning is one of the best known of the Edge Hill sculptures. In the tradition of Henry Moore it was originally on show at the Crystal Palace. Constructed from preformed concrete, at first sight it seems to be two separate parts, closer inspection reveals that it *is* two separate parts, but linked. This gave the title 'Eternal Struggle' and, in a burst of irony (?), it was located outside the Chief Executive's window! Another favourite sculpture is *Embargo* by the late Ted Roocroft. This is a sculpture of a group of humans huddled together. Ted was a well-known visitor to Edge Hill where he had given practical demonstrations of his craft, particularly during Arts Week in 1989. Tom Titherington, Head of Art, paid this tribute to him:

> He carved and talked in a sunny spot outside the Art and Design block as the lovely sheep, which was eventually exhibited in the library, gradually emerged. He delighted in his calling and his

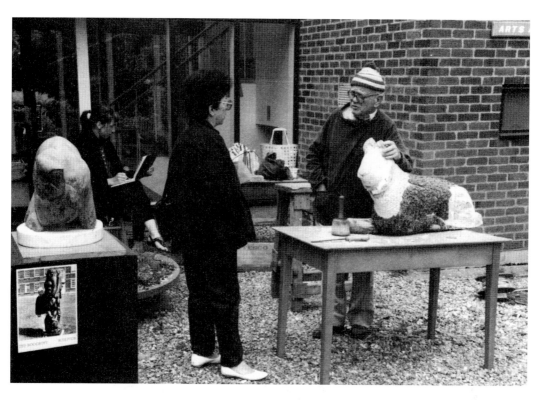

57    *Sculptors at work, with artists in residence: Chris Kowal-Post and Ted Rookcroft.*

**58**   *Green Arts Week*

work clearly expressed his delight. Looking at Ted carving made you marvel. All the subtlety and willingness of his feelings towards the material and the world around him was embodied in the movement when the chisel met the wood.[1]

Edge Hill is also concerned to display student work. *Family* was one of a series of sculptures by Helen Juste. Helen's work as a nurse inspired her to create the clay sculpture.

I was able to observe lots of different families visiting their sick relatives. Over a period of time I became fascinated by the complex dynamics visible within each family group. This fascination resulted in my series of sculptures exploring these unique relationships in a visual form.[2]

Being an educational establishment, Edge Hill wished to develop the park as a resource for schools and for the wider community. Schoolchildren were encouraged to visit and take part in workshops. Joint funding by Edge Hill and Merseyside Arts enabled the institution to provide two residencies: that of Ted Roocroft (14-18 May 1990) and Christine Kowal Post (21-25 May 1990). Christine carved and painted two cherubs which were go to Oldham Art Gallery. She described how she did her work:

I usually rough out large carvings with a small chainsaw and draw directly on the plank or log without making preparatory drawings. A 'thumb nail' sketch is usually all I need because when I use my chisels I am drawing onto and into the wood, and eventually the carving itself takes over.

A carving may take a few months to complete, a small carving just a couple of weeks. If I am going to use colour to define forms I normally use oil paints diluted with turpentine.

*59*   *Bingo Bango*

This meant that the general public could see and talk with sculptors at work. Also provided were two Raku workshops and two wood sculpture workshops. Further contributions to the 1990 Merseyside Visual Arts Festival included 'Head over Hills', an exhibition of ceramic sculpture, reliefs and drawings by Marjan Wouda, a Dutch-born sculptor. 'Fragments of animals and landscape, pulled up from the raw matter of the earth, are about to be returned to it. Thus the work encompasses the themes of death and decay as well as that of becoming.'

Edge Hill was also keen to develop multi-racial cultural links and cross-institutional arts activities. *Intonations* was founded in September 1993 to promote traditional and modern artworks from non-European cultures. An exhibition of African artworks by artists from the Oshobo school in Western Nigeria was displayed, the proceeds of which went to the artists. On 1 October 1993 a stunning exhibition of works (from non-European cultures) was organised by the Afro-Asian Studies and the Art & Design departments and the Black Students Caucus group. To quote Dr. Jenny Clegg from Afro-Asian Studies, 'We felt it was important to show traditional art forms, representations of the great cultural wealth of non-western civilisations, as well as works of modern international standing. At the same time, we worked to create opportunities for local artists from non-European backgrounds so that their work might become better known'.[3] Exhibitors included Wang Jianan, who had trained at Beijing Central Academy of Fine Arts and in 1986 opened the first independent arts studio in China since the Cultural Revolution he also had been awarded the Royal Academy Watercolour Prize in 1989); Edmund To (originally from Hong Kong), who runs the Taoist Studio in Manchester, a centre for Chinese printing, calligraphy and meditation; Karen Babayou, who though part-Armenian was brought up in Iran, and Paul Clarkson from Liverpool. Traditional artefacts from Africa and Asia and embroideries from Bangladesh and India were also on show. The exhibition aroused a lot of interest and demonstrated the rich variety of artistic talent available in the non-European world.

Edge Hill was thus making a determined effort to demonstrate that culture should not be seen as Eurocentric. Equal Opportunities also put on a series of workshops by acclaimed artists like Moy McCrory. Equally there is concern to promote full accessibility for the local community as a whole. The Rose Theatre, after refurbishment and with the backing of the North West Arts Council, has put on the work of disabled artists and the Drama Department has also been involved in disabled arts work. Since 1993 the Rose Theatre has been concerned to stage a programme of Drama, Dance and Mime. This has been supported by the North West Arts Board and Lancashire County Council. A 'World Beat' music programme was its first project. In the summer of 1994, Edge Hill staged its first open access community performance, 'Electric Carmina Burana'. Drawing its performers from the wider community and not just Edge Hill University College, this involved music, drama and dance.

Following this was perhaps one of Edge Hill's most ambitious projects, that of its Green Arts Week held from 27 June to 1 July 1995. The centrepiece was 'Cry of the Earth', composed by Edge Hill's Head of Music, Tony Biggin. This had been premièred at the Royal Festival Hall in 1990. It was a piece of music theatre designed to draw attention to conservation and the future of the planet. Since it involved not only music but also dance, drama and the visual arts, a wide range of departments, along with representatives from West Lancashire arts and environmental organisations, took part in what was another open access project.

Green Arts Week also hosted exhibitions, talks, a community arts day, a schools' day and a procession through Ormskirk. Schools and organisations were encouraged to write a green

**60**   *'The Gates of Greenham'*

pledge or manifesto detailing what they would do to help conserve or improve the environment over the next year. On 26 June, the pledges were carried to Edge Hill in a large procession accompanied by music. A tunnel was constructed from parade items linking an environmental exhibition in the LRC with the Rose Theatre (where the performances of 'Cry of the Earth' took place). The week was a great success—the rural campus was ideal for such a production—and did raise environmental awareness, though whether it will have a lasting effect is difficult to determine. 'Cry of the Earth', however, attracted such attention that the cast and choir were invited to stage a repeat performance in Leiden in the Netherlands in April 1996. This was another highly successful and satisfactory event. In June 1996 'Gates of Greenham', inspired by the Women's Peace Camp, was staged, again as a full community project. Two new pieces have been commissioned by Edge Hill University College for 1997; 'Unseen' (music, Tony Biggin and librettist, Phil Christopher), which deals with human rights issues, and 'Bestiale' about animal rights (music, Tony Biggin, librettist, John Simons).

The Rose Theatre also staged a music recital programme and literary events. Well-known names such as Royal National Theatre and Compas have appeared there as have new companies such as Doo Cot and Fish Pool Dance Company. Edge Hill University College is constantly trying to widen the audience for Arts especially within the local community. With this in mind, Edge Hill is bidding for lottery money to develop an Arts Centre on the present site of the Rose Theatre. Already it has been awarded funds by the Arts Council for an architectural competition to draw up a range of possible schemes.

*61*    *Drama*

## II **Sports Facilities**

Edge Hill made a successful lottery bid for £1,711,813 to help provide a sports complex which would serve not only the institution, but also the West Lancashire community (the balance of funding of £1.6m was provided by Edge Hill). Facilities include: all-weather floodlit tennis courts, multi-courts and hockey pitches, six-lane athletics track up to county standard, rugby, soccer and cricket pitches, additional PE laboratory and fitness suite, a new sports pavilion and additional car parking. Floodlighting means that the complex can be used at night and there are facilities for the disabled. This is testimony to the high regard in which sport and sports studies at Edge Hill are held. The sports development is built on land leased from local landowners (an initiative first suggested by Ruth Gee, who had seen the need for more space but had been unable

62    *John Cater receives lottery money.*

63    *Mike Atherton opening Sporting Edge.*

64     *Hi-tech gym*

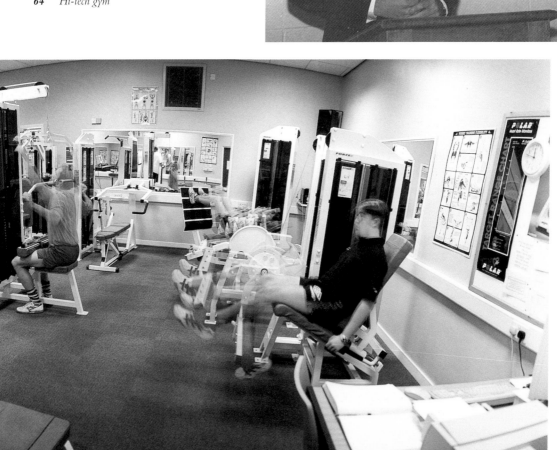

**65**   *Sports hall*

to secure it on sufficiently favourable terms) behind Forest Court. This development is typical of Edge Hill's desire to provide the best—the aim is to produce a centre of excellence—not just for its own academic community but also to contribute to the wider regional community. It is the first complex of its kind to be offered for public use in West Lancashire.

## III **Edge Hill Enterprises**

One of the new appointments needed by Incorporation was that of Marketing Manager. Michael Frain was appointed to this post in 1989. He came to Edge Hill from a background of private education. His previous position had been as director of Lansdowne College, an Anglo-American College in London. Prior to that he had been chief executive of a national training institute, principal of an international college at Norwich and consultant in staff training at Singapore Polytechnic. His initial task at Edge Hill was to ensure a higher profile for the institution by promoting a corporate image, designing a logo which would signal a clear, consistent message, and co-ordinating press releases as well as generating income from new sources. This latter point was received with some scepticism by many staff but the work of Edge Hill Enterprises from 1992 has confounded such doubts.

Edge Hill Enterprises began trading as a separate company on 1 April 1992. Its work encompasses three aspects, each of which is designed to further the institution's profile and bring in much needed finance. Initially and perhaps most obviously was an attempt to boost income by utilising Edge Hill's resources to a greater extent. The campus was only being used for seven and a half months a year so it was sensible to try to develop further the conference trade. A realistic approach was used. There was no point in trying to attract large international companies because accommodation was not good enough. Instead Mike Frain, building on his earlier work as Marketing Manager, worked at developing a niche market in social, leisure and educational facilities. This has proved very successful and employs some 150 people. Many organisations also come for conferences.

Allied to this are the international activities based largely in America. This market has again been successfully developed. Edge Hill maintains an office in Texas staffed by Michael Clarke (who used to be International Marketing Manager at the Ormskirk Campus). Edge Hill has partner arrangements with up to thirty American universities. This yields around one hundred students for Edge Hill courses who are looked after by Edge Hill Enterprises. New projects have also been developed with American universities. Thus the American MBA resulted from links with Oklahoma City University, one of America's most international universities. The degree is accredited by The North Central Association which is responsible for validating almost 1,000 colleges in Central America. Oklahoma has links with Singapore, Hong Kong, Peking, Kuala Lumpur, as well as Ormskirk, and it is expected that students from all these countries will participate. In three years, numbers on this programme have increased from 10 to one hundred and fifty. This has brought students from India, Turkey, Pakistan, Oklahoma, Singapore, Taiwan and Korea. The European Union also agreed to fund British students on the MBA course. This means that British students are taught by American and British professors at Ormskirk and awarded an American degree. This brings not only international students to Ormskirk, but also internationally renowned professors. Edge Hill also bids for EU money for projects in areas like Greece, Cyprus and Turkey. In 1995 it was awarded a European Union contract to lead a training project in these countries to establish training offices and deliver training for local government staff.

One of Enterprises' most successful operations is that of UK training, backed by funds from the EU Social Fund. One hundred people are employed in this area, with 25 full-time trainers who have experience in areas of local need, e.g. marketing, tourism, computers, theatre. They train the unemployed, small companies to enable them to develop further and large companies to bring more money into the region. Barclaycard, Airtours, Everton Football Club, Granada and the BBC have all had training from Enterprises. Much of the training is done at the Aintree site where a new training area has been constructed. Other projects include industrial tourism. Training projects are set up to help local companies to see if there could be a market for the trappings of tourism. One example of this was Cain's brewery which now has a pub, a guided tour and a visitors' centre all based on the training received from Edge Hill Enterprises. All of this ensures that the institution receives a much higher regional profile.

Enterprises also provides some unique projects. Court Reporting was the first of these. It was designed as a response to the fact that over 300 of England's Crown Courts were to be converted to computer-aided transcription. This was a system whereby computerised shorthand could appear immediately in formatted English on a monitor. Edge Hill collaborated with Educorp International from Texas who were already providing the system in America. Its benefits were not confined to the law courts,

**66**  *Statue*

however; it could also be used at conferences (particularly where many languages were being spoken), in television and as an aid for those of impaired hearing. Employment prospects were good and it was hoped that it would prove of particular interest to women wishing to return to work, the disabled and those from ethnic groupings, thereby again advancing the institution's mission to wider access. It thus has great advantages in providing equal opportunities in the teaching situation. It has provided facilities for a hearing impaired student from one of Edge Hill's American partner institutions.

Edge Hill Enterprises is an extremely successful concern. Further projects are constantly being floated, such as work with Israeli universities in connection with management and training. It has raised the institution's profile internationally and it is very useful in contributing to the cost of running Edge Hill.

## IV  **Partnerships**

**67**  *Early years*

Within the educational sphere, much attention has been given to the idea of partnership. As well as the partnership agreements with local schools and the Lancashire Project,[4] links with local FE colleges have been fostered. These foundation years' arrangements have been in place since 1992 with Knowsley Community College, Nelson & Colne College, Skelmersdale College, Southport College, St Helens College, Wigan and Leigh College, whereby Edge Hill offers a four-year degree place to students wishing to take certain named degrees, who successfully qualify after studying for their first year, in one of the above designated colleges on a validated access course. A special arrangement was also in operation until 1995 with Wigan Metropolitan College offering places on Edge Hill's Geography and

**68**   *The grounds*

Field Biology and Habitat Management degrees. In addition, special franchising arrangements have been successfully held with Skelmersdale College since 1993 whereby certain Part I modules have been undertaken at Skelmersdale, students then transferring to Edge Hill for Part II. At Halton College, Part I of the BA modular scheme has been franchised on a part-time basis along with post registration modules with the School of Health Studies. Edge Hill is very conscious of new developments like GNVQ and is particularly interested in developments like progression from GNVQ into Primary Teaching. Partnership is seen as one of the ways forward for the future.

## v   Teacher Education

Although teacher education now counts for little over a third of Edge Hill's activity, it still remains very important. It is perhaps the area most vulnerable to government control and targets, and in the last decade has had to adapt to policies which could change many times in one year. The Council for the Accreditation of Teacher Education (CATE) has been succeeded by the Teacher Training Agency (TTA). The Budget of November 1996 provides the most recent example of change of direction. This caused the Teacher Training Agency to change its recruitment targets for the third time in less than a year. In January 1996 steady growth was required, by the summer this had become rapid growth but now is to be a decline as far as primary is concerned, while secondary is to be levelled off. This means that, instead of primary numbers growing by 26 per cent over the next three years, they will be cut by six per cent, while the projected increase in secondary places of 30 per cent will now be limited to two per cent growth. John Cater, as chairman, of the Standing Conference of Principals' teacher education sub-group, pointed to the entire sector's dismay:

> We were horrified to discover that we had yet another big shift in intake targets. For less well-off institutions which are heavily involved in initial teacher training this could mean they will be left in a very vulnerable position.[5]

**69**   *Sculpture*

It is impossible to describe all changes in great detail, but the major shifts in national policy and the responses to them by Edge Hill, both for primary and secondary education, will be considered.[6]

On 23 November 1993 the Government issued Circular 14/93, *The Initial Training of Primary School Teachers: New Criteria for Courses*. This superseded DES Circular 24/89. Circular 14/93 set out the knowledge and skills which new teachers were to have and required students to spend a greater proportion of their time in schools, not just as an extension of traditional teaching practice but actively implementing course delivery. This meant that courses had to be planned and delivered in partnership with schools. From September 1994 any new primary courses had to meet the new criteria, while all existing courses had to be revised in accordance with them by September 1996.

This occasioned a vast expansion in the role of schools in teacher education. Student teachers were to spend longer in the school classroom which resulted in fewer hours at the institutions. Courses were to be delivered through school-based work and teachers had to be involved to a greater extent in course planning and delivery. Richard Foster, then Head of Teacher Education, was sceptical about the supposed benefits of these proposals, seeing them as an attempt to create teachers on the cheap, and as a threat to quality:

> Mr. Patten had been attempting to train teachers to carry out a series of mechanistic tasks in the classroom, whilst what we are providing at Edge Hill is based on an understanding of the nature of childhood. There is all the difference in the world between a technician who is able to perform a series of functions in the classroom and somebody else who has a profound understanding of the needs of children. Our reputation is in teacher education and not teacher training—there's a subtle but important difference between the two.[7]

Nevertheless Edge Hill had already been building links with local education authorities and headteachers and therefore was in a position to implement a full partnership scheme.

*70   Cosmopolitan Group 3.*

Indeed DFE Circular 9/92 had stated that 'schools should play a much larger part in ITT as full partner of higher education institutions' and Edge Hill had had 'partnership agreements' with a growing number of local schools for several years. A series of regional meetings with staff and headteachers was held in the summer of 1994. This was extended through a year of policy development and pilot work in schools, so that Edge Hill was ready to implement the new procedures in September 1996. To work effectively, a whole new range of competencies had to be created. Teachers would have to be given support and training to enable them to do likewise. A mentoring role was vital: 'Mentors are the key feature in the effective development of student teachers'.[8] Again, Edge Hill was well placed to provide this. Edge Hill tutors took this on in addition to their normal activities and provided mentoring training schemes. The mentor took responsibility for students' work undertaken during periods of school-based training; he/she acted as a key link between the school and Edge Hill, oversaw the student teacher's planning, supervised the student during the 'Block Professional Experience', assessed the student's attainment, provided guidance and liaised with the class teacher, headteacher and college link tutor. This was obviously a key management position and it is not surprising to find that many mentors, particularly in secondary schools, went on to promoted posts.

As well as a mentor who represented the school side of the partnership, a 'link tutor' was provided by Edge Hill. The link tutor's job was two-fold: liaison (between the school and Edge Hill, as a point of contact for students, with the mentors) and Quality Assurance. Throughout the partnership, the aim is to produce exactly that—a partnership—not an imposition from Edge Hill. All aspects of the partnership are equally and vitally necessary. The group of link tutors has become almost a management group.

Despite initial reservations, this has proved to be a successful development which has brought advantages to all concerned. Freda Bridge identified the following benefits for schools: the enhancement of pupil learning, increase in staffing, ability to concentrate on special needs pupils, opportunities for research and development in schools, professional development of staff, extra funding, opportunity to reflect upon existing practice, development of relationships between colleagues, students and institutions, use of ITE materials and skills in other areas of the school's life, opportunity to be involved in clusters and mentoring networks, new materials, new ideas, younger teachers in school, common induction with newly qualified teachers (NQT), help with the development of induction programmes for NQTs, enhanced position with the rest of staff, career opportunities. Students gained 'wide ranging experiences of the full range of non-classroom activities—special needs, assessment, pastoral care, parental involvement, motivating youngsters, adolescence and classroom management' and the 'ultimate beneficiaries are the pupils in school'.[9]

Developments in secondary teaching mirrored to a large extent those in primary. Again mentoring is vital. Students have a professional mentor who has overall responsibility for all trainee teachers within the individual schools—a curriculum mentor responsible for trainees within a particular subject area and a link tutor who provides quality assurance and support for the school. Despite initial uncertainties on both the school's and Edge Hill's sides, this has worked well. Edge Hill has seen a vast increase in secondary provision over the last few years: it is now the eighth largest provider in the country. This is a remarkable achievement, given that the institution is in fierce competition with other local providers.

# 12
# THE FUTURE

Ruth Gee was succeeded by Dr. John Cater who became acting Chief Executive in the summer of 1993, a position which was confirmed in January 1994. A well-known academic in his own right, having written numerous publications on public policy as well as being co-author of a best selling geography text, John had come up through the ranks. He had originally joined Edge Hill as a lecturer in geography in 1979, then became Head of Urban Policy, Co-ordinating Head of Department, Deputy Dean of the former HESS faculty, Head of Policy, Planning & Development and Director of Resources. John was keen to emphasise that, though conditions were becoming ever more harsh with cutbacks in funding, Edge Hill was still in a good position to continue to progress. Its budget had been effectively managed and it was felt that appropriate systems were in place to ensure further good quality.

*71   Dr. John Cater*

> Now is the time to keep the flow of ideas coming: and to develop breadth from our existing programmes by, for instance, using our modular structures in the most effective way possible.[1]

He is fully committed to the institution's mission statement of openness, honesty and trust. Edge Hill has an open, accessible and positive working atmosphere. 'It's a good place to work and study, and I think we need to build on these strengths we already have to foster a sense of real ownership among both staff and students'.[2] John sees his job as one of helping people realise their potential.

## I  Management and Quality Assurance

In the new climate of accountability, it is necessary to demonstrate how quality and responsibilities are operated. Documentary evidence of processes is vital. Mark Flinn was appointed as Director of Academic Affairs and Quality Management in 1992. His brief is twofold: to overview the Schools (which now number five, Humanities and Arts; Health Studies; Science and Technology; Social Sciences and Management; and Education), and the ways in which the curriculum is delivered and to assure the quality of what is done. This is extremely important especially in times of diminishing resources. How are academic standards maintained? How can a secure future for Edge Hill be ensured?

As the institution matured, a reassessment of Edge Hill's relationship with the University of Lancaster was required. Despite the fact that the University obviously valued Edge Hill, the relationship had not really progressed in the sense that the course consultants could still freeze development. Validations took place at Lancaster but did not involve proper peer exchange of views. Rapid staff development on validation at Edge Hill to bring Edge Hill staff up to scratch produced people willing to offer constructive criticism about others' courses. By the end of 1994, Edge Hill had won accreditation, meaning that validation took place on the Edge Hill campus. A formal process of programme review and re-validation was instituted, all of which won praise when the HEQC Quality Audit took place in January 1996. As part of its review, it had to:

(i) consider and review the mechanisms and structures used by … institutions … to monitor, assure, promote and enhance their academic quality and standards, in the light of their stated aims and objectives.

(ii) comment on the extent to which such procedures in place in individual institutions reflect appropriate good practice in maintaining and enhancing quality, and are applied effectively.[3]

After an exhaustive audit from 23-25 January 1996, during which 220 staff and students met the Audit Team, Edge Hill was delighted to receive a highly favourable report in which it was commended for many good practices and aspects of quality assurance.

The initial euphoria of the Quality Audit's positive verdict was quickly tempered by the realisation that, if the institution was to move forward, then attention had to be paid to the areas designated as needing 'minor' improvement. Accordingly, Mark Flinn set to work to monitor and improve further the quality of Edge Hill's provision by developing a Quality Enhancement Framework. This will enable staff to reflect and appraise existing provision while developing relevant performance indicators and action plans. It is an attempt to be ready for the new Quality Agency which will take over from HEQC and the Quality Assessment functions of HEFCE. That quality is constantly being improved is evidenced by the 'excellent' rating achieved by Communication Studies in the HEFCE assessment of 2-5 December 1996.[4] Edge Hill also hopes to achieve an 'Investors in People' Award in 1998 (the School of Health Studies received this in 1995). Such an award will again demonstrate commitment to quality.

## II Research

Since the mid-1970s, Edge Hill has developed a staff profile with a strong research capacity. As with other institutions in the (then) PCFC sector, however, Edge Hill was not able to benefit from the large amounts of funding granted to the pre-1992 universities for research. Originally allocated as a block grant by the UGC, this research funding became increasingly selective and was informed by a major Research Assessment Exercise (RAE), taking place every four years. Although eligible to enter the 1992 RAE, Edge Hill chose not to do so, and focused its energies on the development of the LRC and on the IT network.

Nevertheless, by 1995, Edge Hill had developed a number of strong areas of research activity. Pre-eminent amongst them was the Centre for Studies in Crime and Social Justice (CSCSJ) which, under the leadership of Professor Phil Scraton, has developed an

**72** *Detail of building façade*

international reputation in critical criminology and social justice and produced key publications on policing, imprisonment, controversial deaths, disaster analysis, childhood, gender and sexuality. Perhaps its best known work is that on the Hillsborough football disaster of 1989 where 96 people died. This is a long-term project funded by Liverpool City Council and has four main foci: official responses to the disaster including the reception of the bereaved; media intervention and the impact of intrusive journalism; the legal procedures and their impact on the bereaved/ survivors; the role of the police and inter-agency conflict. From this has developed further research on other disasters such as the *Marchioness* pleasure cruiser, 1989 (51 dead) and the Zeebrugge ferry disaster, 1987 (193 dead).

The Centre offers two highly successful part-time M.A. degrees in Crime, Deviance and Social Policy and Human Rights and Equal Opportunities, a full doctoral programme as well as several active research groups. They include: Disasters and their Aftermath; Health Care in Prisons; Gender and Sexuality; Young People; Power and Justice and European Policing. In 1995 HEFCE rated the Centre as 'excellent' in all categories under assessment.

Other inter-disciplinary research centres have been established in Local Policy Studies, Development and Environmental Studies, Health Care and Evaluation (see above in Health Studies) and Mentoring (see above, Woodlands). The Centre for Local Policy Studies, as its name implies, is concerned with all aspects of policy, organisation and management at the local and sub-national level occurring both in Britain and internationally. It promotes research, publications and consultancy with local authorities/community organisations.

ICDES stands for the International Centre for Development and Environmental Studies whose work focuses mainly on third world development and environmental issues. It publishes an international newsletter *Common Ground* funded by the Danish Government and has provided a short course/consultancy training programme to assist inner-city environmental improvement at Sheffield as well as a number of staff development workshops in Denmark. All of these centres help to raise the profile of the institution both nationally and internationally.

In the 1996 RAE, four of the units of assessment entered by Edge Hill, received ratings indicating work of national excellence, and two of them (Social Policy and Administration, and History) were given ratings strong enough to guarantee financial support from the Funding Council for a four-year period. By this stage, planning for the next RAE, expected in 2000, had already started.

★　★　★

Despite the extension of 'consolidation' till 1999, and the continuing downward pressure on the unit of resource, Edge Hill is determined:

(i)   to continue to diversify its academic provision;

(ii)  to ensure that its students are equipped both as academic graduates and with a range of skills which will allow them to contribute fully to society;

(iii)  to support and contribute to the life of local and regional communities, not just in terms of education but also in respect of social and cultural activities. Further diversification of academic provision will be undertaken by developing Continuing Vocational Education and making part-time provision more consistent with student demand.

It has emphasised these points in its response to the National Committee of Enquiry into Higher Education (Dearing Inquiry) and also signalled its concern that the Quality Assurance arrangements for teacher education differ from the rest of the Higher Education sector.

The big decision, however, is whether or not Edge Hill goes for taught Degree-Awarding Powers (DAP). Taught DAP have many obvious attractions. They are a measure of an institution's academic maturity; they are one of the current criteria for university status (and therefore essential should Edge Hill ever decide to seek full university status); they may perhaps become one of the formal criteria for the confirmation of university college status which would enable Edge Hill to stand apart from the FE sector. Objective HEQC reporting demonstrates that quality assurance systems and processes function well, though HEQC officials suggested that the continuing level of Lancaster's involvement in course validation (which is perceived as being higher than the 'norm' in accredited institutions) might obscure the fact that Edge Hill does have its own successful independent systems. Accordingly, Edge Hill has formally approached Lancaster University requesting a change in the need for observers and the role of its standing committee. Should this go well, a bid for DAP will be made. This would obviously impact on Edge Hill's relationship with Lancaster University because, if Edge Hill were successful in gaining the powers, Lancaster might wish Edge Hill to use them. At present Edge Hill would prefer to gain the powers but continue its accredited relationship with Lancaster, since it feels this would benefit Edge Hill, Lancaster University and the region as a whole. Roehampton and the University of Surrey have followed this model and found it to be satisfactory.

Edge Hill is also keen to develop its marketing strategies in a much wider sense than previously. Rhiannon Evans, who was formerly Head of the College Services Faculty at Wirral Metropolitan College, was appointed Director for Students and Marketing in 1994. Working with John Cater, Mark Flinn and a revamped Marketing and Communications Unit under Barbara Smith, she has brought a new approach to marketing.

While aware that the institution had many strengths—in the way it was led, in its mission, its commitment to values and its previous good developmental work, particularly in IT—Rhiannon was aware of marketing weakness in that there was no corporate marketing strategy. It is important therefore that marketing is seen not just as advertising, particularly in the sense of producing the prospectus and other glossy brochures, but as Barbara Smith says:

> This is only one small part of the story. Marketing comes into virtually everything we all do. Not merely in how we promote Edge Hill, but also in an approach that puts the student at the centre of everything. We all need to be 'part-time marketeers' and to consider how our role fits into a marketing framework.[5]

Marketing has now been established as an important management function and steps have been taken to ensure that all staff realise they have a vital role to play. The institution as a whole has to network. With this in mind, Edge Hill has a strategic plan in place for the next three years, designed to promote Edge Hill nationally as well as in the locality and the region, and to raise awareness of Edge Hill as a 'major provider of a wide range of higher education courses'.[6] John Cater, in one of his many roles, as Chairman of the Standing Conference of Principals' Teacher Education Sub-group, is working to ensure a national profile. This is important as Edge Hill cannot be easily categorised: it is not a Church foundation, it has never amalgamated with an FE institution, it is generalised not specialised. What it does have is a portfolio of interesting, well constructed courses, many of which are not available in similar institutions. The aim is to ensure that Edge Hill remains a high quality, financially secure institution, with good recruitment and retention. In this way, it should have no difficulty in surviving in the post-Dearing era.

**73**   *Sporting Edge, opened May 1997*

**74** *Skipping*

# APPENDIX I

# THE HOME READING ASSOCIATION

When formed in June 1889, the Home Reading Association had two objects: to encourage the habit of regular reading of 'such books as will not merely please, but educate'; and to maintain contact between former students and Edge Hill. Sixty-four people had enrolled by the time of the first meeting in June 1989 and 22 attended. Meetings were to take place three times a year on Saturdays at 6.00 p.m., one of which was to be of a social nature.

The books chosen were certainly improving. For 1889 these were: Locke, *The Conduct of Understanding*, Tennyson, *In Memoriam*, Kingsley, *Hypatia*, Shakespeare, *Henry V*, Souvestre, *Le Philosophe sous les Toits*, and Carlyle, *French Revolution* Book 1. Members had to read the books and, if requested, write papers on the chief topics. The annual subscription was 5p. At the first meeting Miss Yelf read a paper on *In Memoriam*.

Despite such 'weighty' choices the association appeared popular and by 1892 a surplus of £5 from subscriptions was in hand. It was decided to use this to start a Magazine which would be sold to students at 9d. (3.5p). This became *Edge Hill College Magazine*. Members were expected 'not merely' to 'read the appointed books, but write essays, raise discussions, and ask and answer questions upon difficult points in them'. Its aims were high and were in the best self-help traditions:

> If the guild is to fulfil its purpose which is to encourage the study of literature, and so to widen our sympathies, enlarge our sphere of thought, and lift us up to higher levels than where our *own* poor wisdom would leave us, we must *each one* realise the necessity for self-help and individual effort.[1]

By 1893 the price of the *Magazine* was increased to 5p and its sale was 'very limited'.[2] How popular the Home Reading Association actually was is difficult to determine. Miss Hale obviously had reservations: 'The Home Reading Association flourishes, though I think its members might take more active interest in its work, and so make it more beneficial to themselves and others'. Given the type of book chosen, the hard working day endured by the teachers, the time of meeting—*Saturday* evening—it certainly called for extreme dedication to give up free time.

Though the number of members steadily increased—by 1896 there were over 200— enthusiasm was clearly lacking: 'No essays have been written this year, and no topics have been brought forward for discussion … The Society is not as helpful as it might be, and it is, therefore, hoped that members will become more vigorous'.[3] Whether they became 'more vigorous' is unknown. There was, however, a small number who were fully committed to the Association, and they ensured its continuation into the 20th century. Its offshoot, the *Edge Hill College Magazine*, did flourish to become a forum for the discussion of important questions of the day, as well as a means of keeping former students in touch with developments at Edge Hill. It has certainly proved invaluable in the writing of this history.

# APPENDIX II
# EDGE HILL COLLEGE GUILD
# 1896 - 1997

Both Edge Hill and HMIs were keen that links with former students were to be encouraged and fostered. Accordingly a reunion was held 4 June 1892 attended by 160 old students and many more guests. The dining room was used as a reception room, the lecture room as a dining room, the assembly room as a theatre and the new room for a promenade concert. All were decorated in Edge Hill colours (purple, yellow and green) and each lunch guest received a tiny bouquet of yellow and purple pansies. Mr. S.G. Rathbone, President of the College Council, presided over the lunch and Professor Rendall of University College, Liverpool gave an address. Musical and dramatic recitals and tea rounded off the day.

A second gathering took place on 29 June 1895. The response to invitations was so great that a marquee was needed to hold all the guests. Four hundred people took lunch including a number of 'notables' in education. The secretary of the Education Department, Sir George Kebewick and Mr. Scott Coward, H M Inspector of Training Colleges, both addressed the gathering.

The culmination of all this was the inauguration on 27 June 1896 of the Edge Hill College Guild. Its objects were to help members in time of difficulty, promote sociability via concerts, picnics and other entertainments and strengthen the ties between the institution and former students. Before the end of its first year, 197 had joined and branches were active in Yorkshire and London. By 1910, it had 582 members and had disbursed nearly £175 to help old students in times of need and ill health and had made gifts amounting to £30 to Edge Hill. Further branches were being established. The annual reunion became a highlight of Guild activity which has continued to the present day. The Guild fulfilled a need: delegates reported on their branch activities in each edition of the *Magazine* and their work with hardship cases was particularly welcome at a time when the State provided little help for those in need.

As time progressed, however, it would seem that the Guild held more interest for the older former student than for the present graduate. So much so that the then Warden, Mr. Millins, asked in an open letter in 1969, 'Can its continued existence be justified along its present lines?'. He continued:

> It is painfully obvious that the Guild survives only because of the devotion of a handful of people: Year Members, Branch Secretaries and Chief Officers. Despite strenuous publicity efforts annually the younger generations show no interest in joining. Whilst some members, often of advanced years, gallantly travel long distances year after year to attend branch Meetings, they are in the minority. Such meetings usually attract few people, in proportion to the total number of those who live in the area …
>
> The financial situation remains precarious … The Guild shuffles along on a shoe-string, and on a very tattered shoe-string indeed.

Much, perhaps most, of the secretarial work is carried out by the College, at a time when many other burdens are being laid on our very willing secretaries. In relation to the size of the College and to its many commitments in both initial and in-service training, our secretarial establishment is not generous …

It has been my consistent policy to foster the activities of the Guild. I should be happy to do so in the future. But do people really want it to survive?[1]

A trenchant criticism and one ably answered by Ethel Beckett (1905-6):

… the Guild was not designed to provide excitement, nor are its affairs trivial. It is a quiet thing, instituted … for the mutual help and support of its members, and through the years it has endeavoured to follow this ideal. It is a binding force, welding all together by memories of an association and affection engendered in College years. In their youth few young people feel any need for such a bond. I feel that it is in our later years when one's circle of friends inevitably grows smaller, that memories of that association and affection become a solace. I feel there are many in that state or approaching it, who, though not opposed to change, would be distressed if the structure of the Guild were to be altered beyond recognition, and, while ever looking forward, can still look back to the past, but not live in it.[2]

It is regrettable but true that the Guild has not attracted the contemporary graduate. Nevertheless it continues to take a very active interest in Edge Hill's affairs and 50 people attended the Annual Reunion in 1996; its help has proved invaluable in the preparation of this history.

## Alumni Association

In an attempt to continue an association to enable former students to keep in touch, an Alumni Association was formed in 1991. First directed by Alex Fruin, this is now under the direction of Simon Brew, full-time Alumni Officer. The Alumni Association produces a newsletter, *Leading Edge*, twice a year and a programme of 10- and 25-year reunions held on the same day, which usually cater for around 100 former students. The aim is to build up a significant programme for alumni which will enable former staff and students to keep in touch. Already an Alumni Art Group exists and it is hoped that more will get off the ground.

# APPENDIX III
# THE COLLEGE SONG

This was written in 1907 by Maud Mitchell, then a third-year student. It was sung to the tune 'Glorious Devon'.

*Verse 1*
Once was a College grim and staid
Hard by the roaring sea,
Filled with many a pretty maid
Fair as fair could be,
Each one had her own little say
And each one said it bravely
And cheerfully they pulled one way
As each to each would say

*Chorus*
There's Oxford blue and Cambridge blue
There's the white and blue of Liverpool
But of colours great and small
The dearest of them all
Are Helio, are Helio, Green and Yellow.

*Verse 2*
Strong and straight and true and brave,
Many a game they played,
Played in the sun and played in the rain
Nothing their ardour stayed,
Whether they won or whether they lost
The captain's smile shone bright
For well she knew, there were but few
Who for their colours would not fight.

*Chorus*

*Verse 3*
But there comes a time each year
When some must say 'Goodbye'
And it's very hard to keep the tear
From glancing in the eye;
But as in College, so in life
The fight is to the fearless,
We'll fight the fight,
And do the right
And to Alma mater will be true.

# APPENDIX IV
# COLLEGE PRAYER

---

Grant, we beseech Thee, O Lord to all who have trained in this College, the spirit to think and to do always such things as are rightful, that they, leaning only on Thy Heavenly Grace, may evermore be defended by Thy mighty power, and in the faithful discharge of the duties of which Thou has called them may adorn the doctrine of God, our Saviour in all things. Grant this, O Lord, for Jesus Christ's sake.

Amen

# NOTES

## Chapter 1

1. *Board of Education Report* 1912-13, Cd. 7341 (1914), p.5, para 5.
2. The Pupil Teachers System begun in 1846 instituted five-year apprenticeships with an approved teacher for promising boys and girls aged thirteen. A small salary was paid to the pupil teachers and they were examined annually by HMIs. At the age of 18 they had to sit the Queen's Scholarship Examination.
3. Minute Book 1, 22 February 1882.
4. Ibid., 1 April 1890.
5. Ibid., 25 March, 1 April 1890.

## Chapter 2

1. *Edge Hill College Magazine* 15, 1906, p.6.
2. Ibid., 13, 1904, p.20.
3. Minute Book 2, 14 January 1907, 19 March 1907.
4. *Edge Hill College Magazine* 13, 1904, p.5.
5. *Report*, 1906-7.
6. Ibid., 1907-8.
7. Ibid.
8. *Edge Hill College Magazine* 18, 1909, p.16.
9. Ibid., 22, 1913, p.6.
10. Ibid., 13, 1904, p.16.
11. J.B. Thomas, 'The Origins of Teacher Training at University College, Cardiff, *Journal of Educational Administration and History*, XVI (1984), 13.
12. *Edge Hill College Magazine* 17, 1908, p.15.
13. Ibid., 12, 1903, pp.42-3.
14. *Liverpool Courier*, 4 July 1910.
15. Proposal to establish a College, 4 April 1882. Minute Book 1.
16. *Board of Education Report*, 1912-13, Cd. 7341 (1914), p.151, para 272.
17. *Report*, 1911-12, p.4. See also ibid., 1912-13, p.9; 1913-14, p.4.
18. Unlike Hockwell College where only 10 per cent returned to their home area, Michael Heafford, 'Women Entrants to a Teachers' Training College, 1852-60', *History of Education Society Bulletin* 23, Spring 1979, 19.
19. Minute Book 1, 1 April, 4 July 1884, 30 October 1887; Letter Book 1, 28 January 1885.
20. Minute Book 2, 11 December 1905, 11 June 1906.
21. Minute Book 3, 14 June 1910.
22. Ibid., 11 October 1909.
23. Ibid., 8 February 1910; 9 September 1914.
24. Mary Sheppard, student 1909-11. Written reminiscences.
25. Ibid.
26. Successive HMI reports complained of the lack of a practising school under the control of Edge Hill. By 1912, however, the Board of Education considered that this had 'actually proved an advantage since it led to practice in teaching being conducted under new and more natural conditions'. *Board of Education Report* 1912-13, Cd. 7341 (1914), p.26.
27. The *Board of Education Report* for 1912-13, p.24, para 37 commented of training colleges in general: 'The complaint of an old student that they were "sometimes treated like children, sometimes as nuns, sometimes as servant girls", might have been made with equal justice of most boarding schools for young ladies of the day'. Most of Edge Hill's recruits, however, would have had no first-hand knowledge of boarding schools and for many College must have come as a traumatic experience, e.g. Daisy Cowper came from a very poor background, attended a pupil teacher centre for two years (aged 14-16), was a pupil teacher from 16-18 and had to borrow the £25 admission fees in 1908. J. Burnett (ed.), *Destiny Obscure* (1982), p.198.
28. James F. McMillan, *Housewife or Harlot. The Place of Women in French Society 1870-1940* (Brighton, 1984), p.52. I owe this reference to Dr. F.V. Parsons of the University of Glasgow.
29. Dorothy Waid, 'Random Recollections of Edge Hill College Sixty Years Ago', *Newsletter*, 73 (1964), p.8.
30. Ibid.
31. Mary Price and Nonita Glenday, *Reluctant Revolutionaries, A Century of Headmistresses 1874-1974* (1975), p.41.
32. Waid, *op. cit.*
33. *Report*, 1914-15.
34. *Edge Hill College Magazine* 19, 1910, p.75.
35. Ibid.
36. Lindy Moore, *Bajanellas and Semilinas, Aberdeen University and the Education of Women* (Aberdeen University Press, 1991), pp.78-85.
37. *Edge Hill College Magazine* 19, 1910, p.80.
38. Ibid., 3, 1894, p.49.
39. Ibid., 13, 1904, p.45.
40. See below, Chapter 3.
41. *Edge Hill College Magazine* 7, 1908, p.47.
42. Ibid., p.48.
43. Ibid., 21, 1912, p.40.
44. Ibid., 27, 1918, pp.8-9.
45. Ibid., 28, 1919, p.17.

## Chapter 3

1. Interest in current affairs does not appear to have been particularly encouraged. Newspapers do not seem to have been easily available. Mary Sheppard (1909-11) recalled: 'The most daring deed ever done in our year was the opening of a window one Election Night and dropping a halfpenny on a string to a paper boy who tied the "Special Edition" at midnight on to the same string. When we had shut the window we could not read the results—nobody dared to put on the light!' Popular myth had it that Ethel Annakin, who later married Philip Snowden, the Labour Chancellor, used to slip out at night and address meetings of dock labourers; if so, she was certainly adept at avoiding the Edge Hill security system!
2. *Report*, 1914-15, p.9.
3. *Edge Hill Magazine* 25, 1916, p.46.
4. Ibid., 26, 1917, p.7.

5  Ibid., 27, 1918, p.7.
6  Ibid., 28, 1919, pp.33-4.
7  *Report*, 1914-15.
8  *Edge Hill Magazine* 27, 1918, p.8.
9  This is a rather extreme version of her purple prose. 'When at the close of the Session the hearts of all the subjects of our King Emperor, thrilled at the unexpected news of his illness, and feast turned to fast, songs of rejoicing to lamentation, services of thanksgiving to litanies and prayers for His Majesty's speedy recovery, which God in his great goodness and mercy deigned to grant …', Ibid., 11, 1902, p.5. Why they should be 'thrilled' is unknown.
10  Ibid., 9, 1900, p.29.
11  *Edge Hill College Magazine* 21, 1912, p.7.
12  Ibid., 4, 1895, p.6.
13  Ibid., 22, 1913, p.8.
14  Ibid., 15, 1906, p.11.

**Chapter 4**
1  *Edge Hill Magazine* 30, 1921, p.7.
2  Ibid., 31, 1922, p.7; 32, 1923, p.7.
3  Minute Book 4, 9 July 1924.
4  *Edge Hill Magazine* 36, 1927, p.10.
5  Ibid., 37, 1928, p.7.
6  Ibid., 38, 1929, p.8.
7  Miss Smith, Lord Irwin, Councillor Travis-Clegg, ibid., 43, 1934, p.11.
8  See below, ch.10.
9  Minute B 145-34, 14 February 1934.
10  *Edge Hill College Magazine* 19, 1910, p.46.
11  Ibid., 38, 1929, p.9.
12  Ibid., 40, 1931, p.7.

**Chapter 5**
1  A.L. Binns to P.E. Meadon, 29 December 1941.
2  Oral evidence from A.M. Laing.
3  *Edge Hill Newsletter* 51, 1942, p.4.
4  Mary Bancroft (1943-5), *Newsletter*, 1968-9, p.9.
5  Minute B 130/44, 12/6/44.
6  Ibid.
7  Joyce Kenwrick, Lecturer in Education, *Edge*, 1967, p.10.
8  *Edge Hill Newsletter* 51, 1942, p.5; ibid., 52, 1943, p.6.
9  Ibid., 54, 1945, p.7.
10  Ibid., 55, 1946, p.5.
11  Ibid.
12  Ibid., 56, 1947, p.16.

**Chapter 6**
1  *Edge Hill Newsletter* 66, 1957, p.5.
2  Minutes 8/59/57; 11/3/57.
3  Ibid., 31/10/67.
4  Principal's Report, 4/7/64.
5  Ibid.

**Chapter 7**
1  Expansion Proposals in Response to College Letter 7/65. The governors agreed to this on 22 October 1965.
2  Expansion Proposals in Response to College Letter 7/65.
3  G.F. Bartle, *A History of Borough Road College* (Kettering, 1976), pp.96-8.
4  Quoted in G.P. McGregor, *Bishop Otter College and Policy for Teacher Education 1839-1980*, p.208.
5  Principal's Report, February 1972.
6  A new purpose-built library was opened in 1973.
7  Principal's Report, June 1972.
8  Governor's Minutes, 29/6/73.
9  V C to Senate, January 1973 on 'The University and the Colleges of Education'. Principal's Memo 6/73.
10  Director's Report, D/75 Autumn 1975.
11  Director's Report, Summer 1982.

**Chapter 8**
1  Fiona A. Montgomery, *Edge Hill College: a history 1885-1985* (1985), p.73.
2  Bob Wilson, oral evidence, 10/1/97.
3  Tony Woods and Stephen Bunker, *A Hatful of Talent* (University of Luton Press, 1994).
4  See below, ch.9.

**Chapter 9**
1  Ruth Gee, 'Survival is not compulsory' in Susan Weil (ed.), *Introducing Change from the top in Universities and Colleges* (Kegan Paul, 1994), pp.131-40.
2  Harry Webster, *The Education Act, 1988: Statement of Progress*.
3  Ruth Gee, *op. cit.*, p.133.
4  See 'Health Studies', below, pp.71-4.
5  I am grateful to Elizabeth Wiredu for this information.
6  Strategic Plan 1992/93-1995/96, p.8.
7  Ibid.
8  *Edgeways*, April 1996.

**Chapter 10**
1  Data supplied by Touche Ross, as part of a pilot Value for Money study into academic libraries, June 1995, funding by HEFCE.
2  *Talis*, November 1996.
3  HEQC Quality Audit, p.18, para. 18.
4  Ruth Gee, 'Survival is not compulsory'.
5  *Edgeways*, 2 February 1990.
6  Ibid., February 1996.

**Chapter 11**
1  *Edgeways*, October 1991.
2  Ibid., June 1994.
3  Ibid., September 1993.
4  See above, p..
5  *Times Higher*, 6 December 1996.
6  I am grateful to Margaret Entwistle, Freda Bridge and Richard Foster for providing me with information.
7  *Leading Edge*, 6 August 1994, p.6.
8  Freda Bridge, 'Educating Student Teachers—Your Job or Mine?', *Management in Education*, 10, 1 February/March 1996, p.25.
9  Ibid., p.26.

**Chapter 12**
1  *Edgeways*, 4 January 1994.
2  Ibid.
3  HEQC Quality Audit Report, p.3, para 2.
4  This followed on 'excellence' achieved by Applied Social Sciences and the Centre for Studies in Crime and Social Justice.
5  Barbara Smith, 'Marketing News', *Edgeways*, February 1996.
6  End of Year Marketing Report to Governors, June 1996.

**Appendix I**
1  *Edge Hill Magazine*, 1, 1892, p.59.
2  Ibid., 2, 1893, p.50.
3  Ibid., 5, 1986, p.59.

**Appendix II**
1  *Edge*, 1969, p.10.
2  *Newsletter*, 1970.

# BIBLIOGRAPHY

This does not pretend to be a comprehensive list of works available, or consulted, but only of those which proved to be most useful for my purpose.

## A  Primary Sources

*(1)*  *Official*
### (a)  Public Record Office (Kew)

| | |
|---|---|
| Education 17 | Teacher Training |
| 17/56 | |
| 17/57 | |
| 40 | Endowment Files 1858-1945 |
| 40/53 | |
| 40/54 | |
| 40/109 | |
| 78 | Teacher Training College Files 1924-61 |
| 78/28 | |
| 115/28 | |

### (b)  HMI Reports, 1885-1907
*Teacher Training 1805-1890,* P.P. 1914, XXV
*Board of Education Report 1912-13*, Cd. 7341 (1914)
*McNair Report (Training of Teachers and Youth Leaders)*, HMSO, 1944
*Robbins Report, Report of the Committee on Higher Education*, HMSO 1963
*Newsom Report, Report of the Minister of Education's Central Advisory Council*, 'Half Our Future', HMSO, 1963
*Weaver Report, Report of the Study Group on the Government of Colleges*, HMSO, 1972
*Education: A Framework for Expansion*, HMSO, 1972

*(2)*  *Local Material*

| | |
|---|---|
| Minute Books I-IV | 1882-1925 |
| Governors' Minutes | 1933-1968 |
| | 1969-1984 |
| | 1985-1996 |
| Academic Board Minutes | 1985-1996 |
| Staff Meeting Minutes | 1937-1964 |
| *Edge Hill College Magazine* | 1892-1941 |

| | |
|---|---|
| *Edge Hill College Newsletter* | 1942-1965 |
| *Edge* | 1965-1970 |
| Guild Newsletter | 1971-1984 |
| *Report, Balance Sheet, etc.* | 1891, 1894-1920 |
| *Directories* | 1885-1920 |

| | |
|---|---|
| Register of Students | 1885-1925 |
| | 1930-1951 |
| College Roll | 1885-1947 |
| *Edgeways* | |
| *Leading Edge* | |
| Directors' Reports | 1982-1987 |
| Operating Statements | 1995-1996 |
| | 1996-1997 |
| Strategic Plans | 1992-93-1995-96 |
| | 1996-97-1999-2000 |
| HEQC Quality Audit Report | July 1996 |
| Student Charter | 1995-96 |
| Equal Opportunities Policy | |
| Statement and Guidelines | |
| Annual Reports | 1989-1991 |
| Library Services Development Plan | 1993-2000 |
| Salaries Book | |
| Letter Books, I-III (Large sections are illegible) | |
| Registers of Students' Work | 1885-1895 |
| Miscellaneous correspondence with the Board of Education | 1884-1907 |
| *Proposed Enlargement of Edge Hill Training College* | 1990 |
| *The Bazaar Souvenir* | 4, 5, 6 Oct. 1906 |

Howard Barnes (ed.), *Training Colleges for Schoolmistresses* (1891)

**B      Secondary Sources** (Place of publication London unless otherwise stated)

Bartle, G.F., 'Early Applications by Men to the Borough Road Normal College', *History of Education Society Bulletin*, 14, Aut. 1974, 31-41

Bartle, G.F., 'Early Applications by Women Candidates to the Borough Road Normal College', ibid. 18, Aut. 1976, 36-41

Bartle, G.F., *A History of Borough Road College* (Kettering, 1976)

Bennett, D., *Emily Davies and the liberation of Women* (Andre Deutsch, 1990)

Bentley, L., *Educating Women, A Pictorial History of Bedford College, University of London, 1849-1985*

Bergen, B.H., 'Only a schoolmaster; gender, class and the effort to professionalise elementary education in England 1870-1910', *History of Education*, 22, 1982, 1-21

Bridge, F., 'Educating Student Teachers - Your Job or Mine', *Management in Education*, 10, Feb/Mar 1996, 25-6

Burstyn, J., *Victorian Education and the ideal of womanhood* (1980)

Challinor, E.B., *The Story of St Mary's College, Cheltenham* (Cheltenham, 1978)

Copelman, D.M., *London, Women Teachers, Gender, Class and Feminism* (Routledge, 1985)

Dent, H.C., *The Training of Teachers in the United Kingdom* (1962)

Dyehouse, C., *Girls Growing Up in Late Victorian and Edwardian England* (1981)

Eason, T.W., 'Exploring a Dark Continent: the first eighty years at Edge Hill', *Edge*, 1965

Edwards, E., 'The Culture of Femininity in Women's Teacher Training Colleges 1914-1945' in S. Oldfield (ed.), *This Working-Day World* (Taylor & Francis, 1994)

Gee, Ruth, 'Survival is not compulsory' in Susan Weil (ed.), *Introducing Change from the top in Universities and Colleges* (Kegan Paul, 1994), pp.131-140

Glenday, Nonita and Price, Mary, *Reluctant Revolutionaries: A Century of Headmistresses 1874-1974* (1974)

Heafford, M., 'Women Entrants to a Teachers' Training College, 1852-60', *History of Education Society Bulletin*, 23, Spring 1979, 14-21

Hunt, F., *Lessons for Life. The Schooling of Girls and Women 1850-1950* (Blackwell, 1987)

Lawson, J. and Silver, H., *A Social History of Education in England* (1973)

McGregor, G.P., *Bishop Otter College and policy for teacher education 1839-1980* (1981)

Moore, L., *Banajellas & Semilinas, Aberdeen University and the Education of Women* (Aberdeen University Press, 1991)

Masson, M.R. and Simonton, D., *Women in Higher Education Past, Present and Future* (Aberdeen University Press, 1996)

Purvis, J., *A history of women's education in England* (Open University Press, 1991)

Purvis, J., ' "Women's life is essentially domestic, public life being confined to men" (Comte): Separate Spheres and Inequality in the Education of Working-class Women, 1854-1900', *History of Education*, 10, 1981, 227-243

Rich, R.W., *The Training of Teachers in England and Wales during the Nineteenth Century* (1933)

Rose, Martial, *A History of King Alfred's College, Winchester, 1840-1980* (Phillimore, Chichester, 1981)

Sandiford, Peter, *The Training of Teachers in England and Wales* (1910)

Widdowson, Frances, *Going Up into the next Class* (1983)

Woods, Tony and Bunker, Stephen, *A Hatful of Talent* (University of London Press, 1994)

# INDEX

Aldridge, Sue, 80
ASSIST, 67

Bain, Margaret, 53, 55, 56
Balance of Training, 58
Balfour, Alexander, 1
Bantock, Geoffrey, 59
Bingley, 51-3
Board of Governors, 54, 64, 67
Boer War, 40
Burnham Scale, 26
Bursary System, 17
Butterworth, E.M., 51, 52, 53

Cater, J., 93, 98, 101, 104, 105
Centre for Health Research (CHRE), 73
Centre for Studies in Crime and Social Justice
    (CSCSJ), 102-3
Chapman, Tom, 73
Coles, Mary, 82-4
Community Work Organiser, 61
Crosfield, William, 1
Cunnington, Miss, 25

Day Training Colleges, 5
Dewhurst, M.K., 2, 25
Diploma in Higher Education, 59

Edge Hill College
    Alumni Association, 109
    Anglicanism, 16-17
    Bazaar, 10, 11
    Day Students, 6, 54
    Durning Road, 1, 4, 46, 47
    Extensions, 8, 10, 11, 38
    Fees, 3, 38, 44
    Foundation, 1

HMI reports, 8
Liverpool University, 6, 39, 53, 58, 60
Men appointed to staff, 55-6
New building, Ormskirk, 45, 46, 49
Opening, 1
Scholarship List, 18
Staff, 2
Students' ages, 17-18
Students' destinations, 21-5
Students' origins, 16-21
Teaching practice, 27-8
University College, 63
University students, 6-8, 48
Victoria University, 6
Education Acts
    1870, 1, 54
    1902, 15
    1918, 39
    1944, 54
    1988, 66
Education: A Framework for Expansion (1972), 59
Equal Opportunities, 70-1
Evans, Kate (Mrs.), 2, 25, 38
Evans, Rhiannon, 104

Feminism, 34, 38, 42
Fenemore, Mildred, 2, 25
Feuchsel, Harriet D., 2, 25
Flinn, Mark, 101-2, 104
Forest Court, 75
Frain, Mike, 94-5

Gee, Ruth, 65, 66, 68, 70, 78, 82
Greaves, Brian, 61
Guild, 35, 38, 108-9

Hale, Sarah J., 4, 5, 12-16, 19, 25, 26, 28, 34, 35,